The Wordsworth Book of Limericks

The Wordsworth Book of
Limericks

❧

Selected and edited by
Linda Marsh

WORDSWORTH CLASSICS

7

Readers who are interested in other titles from
Wordsworth Editions are invited to visit our website at
www.wordsworth-editions.com

For our latest list and a full mail-order service, contact
Bibliophile Books, 5 Thomas Road, London E14 7BN
TEL: +44 (0)20 7515 9222 FAX: +44 (0)20 7538 4115
E-MAIL: orders@bibliophilebooks.com

This edition published 1997 by Wordsworth Editions Limited
8B East Street, Ware, Hertfordshire SG12 9HJ

ISBN 978-1-85326-490-0

Typeset in Great Britain by Antony Gray
Printed and bound by Clays Ltd, St Ives plc

Contents

❦

Introduction

❦

The limerick, like much of what it celebrates, can easily become addictive. Each one takes seconds to read. You may be drawn (like many before you) to 'read just one more', until dipping moves to browsing, and whole pages are consumed in one go. This vast collection of limericks, containing those which have been written, sung and spoken over a period of nearly two hundred years, shows how they reflect with undiminished accuracy the humour, neuroses and obsessions of our times; and it is easy to see how the metre and rhyming scheme appeal to the poet in all of us. Generally, their readability has something of the enduring quality of nursery rhymes; everyone's heard of them; everyone can recite one. (Indeed, 'Hickory, dickory dock' is an example of both.) Specifically, their licence to address every subject under the sun but most especially relations between the sexes give many of them an X-certificate boost . . . this is a poetic form with a kick in it.

Recognised old favourites get reworded to fit a person or a place, yet the acts described or the issues confronted can remain strangely familiar. New limericks invigorate the old form by such updatings and the repertoire widens to accommodate the feelings of each new age. What could only privately be circulated, too indecent for mainstream taste, springs out perhaps ten years later into public view as moods and perceptions change. The famous Legman (writing in the preface to his two collections) dourly refers to the blurring of sexual differences in 1964, newly christened 'unisex', wondering if 'with the colourless and unvirile people multiplying like skinned rabbits all around us, the limerick may fall dead or disappear tomorrow'. It didn't! Thirty or more so years later it has, if anything, diversified and multiplied. For the limerick has international and eternal appeal. The true nature of the beast, occasionally peering out from under the demure garments with which the (mainly anonymous) writers have sought to render themselves respectable, is untameable. It defies limits of propriety and it reminds us that civilised societies must dig deep to eradicate the violence of prejudice.

The limerick is essentially a story in five lines of verse. There are usually nine beats in lines one, two and five; six beats in lines three and four. The ninth beats in lines one, two and five are accentuated; and this is called 'anapaestic rhythm or foot' – two short syllables and a long. The first line sets the scene and gives us the main character. Edward Lear's 'There was an old man in a tree' is a perfect example. The second line rhymes with the first:

> Who was horribly stung by a bee . . .

The third and fourth lines are shorter, and they rhyme with each other:

> When they said, 'Does it buzz?'
> He replied, 'Yes, it does.

The fifth line rhymes with the first two and produces the climax.

> It's a regular brute of a bee.'

It is most effective when the climax is unexpected, and Lear's limericks differ from later efforts in that quite often his fifth line mirrors his first. What William Baring-Gould in *The Lure of the Limerick* calls 'the sudden swoop' – the twist that makes you smile – is simply absent, and you may find them weak or oddly satisfying, depending on your taste. Lear's fantastical verbal adventures into nonsense were more critically acclaimed the second time around, but both his books mirror the response to life it seems he always had. He described the experience of going to the city to bank the £125 that he earned for the *Book of Nonsense* as probably so unusual for an artist, normally one of society's poorer citizens, that it must explain why 'the whole way from Temple Bar to the Bank was crowded with carriages and people – so immense a sensation did this occurrence make. All the way back it was the same, which was very gratifying.' His kindly, zippy, zany humorous word-inventions thrilled the children of the 1860s and 1870s (most copies have disappeared, dog-eared with loving use) and reprints have continuously appeared.

Lear's gentle books of nonsense (1846 and then 1862) are often considered to contain the first limericks. In fact two important collections were published before that, both anonymous and both known to Lear. *The History of Sixteen Wonderful Old Women* and *Anecdotes of Fifteen Gentlemen* were published in 1821 and 1822 by John Marshal of London. One of the wonderful old women was called 'Towl' – she 'went to sea with an owl' – and she gave Lear the idea for his much-loved 'The Owl and the Pussycat', Robert Cruikshank's illustration pleasing him. The limerick particularly said to have inspired Lear to write his own was the now famous:

> There was a sick man of Tobago,
> Lived long on rice-gruel and sago;
> But at last, to his bliss,
> The physician said this:
> 'To a roast leg of mutton you may go.'

Far from having claimed to have invented the limerick, or even from using it as a term, he wrote that he discovered in it a 'form of verse lending itself to limitless varieties for rhymes and pictures; and thenceforth the great part of the original drawings and verses for the first *Book of Nonsense* were struck off'.

The word 'limerick' officially entered our language in 1898 according to the *Oxford English Dictionary*, when it was defined as 'indecent nonsense verse'. Whether it originated in the drinking songs of Limerick, a town on the banks of the River Shannon in Ireland, it is not known. But it is far from a nineteenth-century phenomenon. We can go back to some very early examples – 'sumer is i-cumen in' (about 1300), which contains this verse:

> Ewe bleateth after lamb,
> Low'th after calve coo;
> Bullock starteth,
> Bucke farteth –
> Merry sing cuckoo!

and later, others such as this, attributed to Elizabeth I (1533–1603):

> The daughter of debate
> Who discord aye doth sow,
>   Hath reaped no gain
>   Where former reign
> Hath taught still peace to grow.

The very beautiful verse by Herrick (1591–1674) is a reminder of how resonantly lyrical these five lines could be:

> Her eyes the glow-worm lend thee,
> The shooting starres attend thee;
>   And the elves also
>   Whose little eyes glow
> Like the sparkle of fire, befriend thee.

and this lyricism is echoed more than a century later in Leigh Hunt's lovely lines in his 'Song to Ceres':

> Laugh out in the loose green jerkin
> That's fit for a goddess to work in.
> With shoulders brown and the wheaten crown
> About thy temples perking.

There is an even earlier find: two researchers, Robert Swann and Frank Sidgwick, found this in the British Museum's Harleian Manuscript of 1322 (it is recorded in their book *The Making of Verse*, 1934) –

> The lion is wondirliche strong,
> & ful of wiles of wo;
>   & wether he pleye
>   other take his preye
> he can not do bot slo [slay].

You can range over the centuries to discover verse which sufficiently moves towards the metre and style of limericks to deserve comparison with what we recognise as limericks today, and various scholars will point to such moments in history as the emergence of the mad songs after the dissolution of the monasteries under Henry VIII, when wandering beggars sang for their living. Legman cites 'Tom o' Bedlam' as the greatest of them, first recorded in Giles Earle's manuscript music book of about 1615 (though maybe decades old by then, he says) and in limerick metre throughout, 'to a tune as haunting as the words':

> From the hagg and hungry Goblin
> That into raggs would rend yee,
> & the spirit that stand's
> by the naked man,
> In the booke of moones defend yee . . .

Satire and the erotic themes in many drinking songs of the seventeenth and eighteenth centuries give a glimpse of the limerick's early potential, but with all its comings and goings, it was the nineteenth century that saw the limerick finally established in the celebrated form that you can see in this book. With Lear and his two anonymous predecessors; with American books such as *Inklings for Thinklings* in 1865 (one of three volumes of limericks, sales proceeds going to injured soldiers of the Civil War); with university students and dons (especially at Oxford and Cambridge) and with the many clergymen all contributing their wit (named and anonymously), it settled in to stay. The poets Swinburne and Rossetti and friends parodied the innocence of Lear's nonsense verse, limericks concealed in prose appeared innocuously in church newspapers and despite much prevalent unease about the best needing to be kept to oral tradition, both the gentle and the ones with a bite, the witty and the ingenius were ineluctably and irrepressibly churned out.

In the early twentieth century, newspapers and periodicals – *Punch* led the way – set up competitions in which prizes were offered for the best, most pungent last line. And how the limerick 'cleaned up its act', turned briefly into nonsense verse and leapt right back again, is due to the influences of all these different people, making it possible for children and the ordinary reading public to read verse in the same form as readers of a more private kind (all conforming to the same standards of metre and rhyme – and wit?). You might say that the limerick went underground, having a rich life in pamphlets and magazines with a limited circulation. Morris Bishop's much-quoted limerick suggests that, without close quarantine, it promptly becomes 'disorderly, drunk and obscene' . . . it naturally degenerates.

Louis Untermeyer says, 'The limerick absorbed solemnities and absurdities, traditional legends and off-colour jokes, devout reflections and downright indecencies, without a quiver or a loss of syllable. It refused to recognise borderlines or any other limits.' The obscenities of such collections as those in *The Cremorne Magazine* of 1882 show the contributors' relish in scatology, sexual aggression and perversion. As I read three editions of this magazine in the British Library, I became aware of a very particular audience for its wares! The serial story linking all three reveals the writer's preoccupations with sexual power and sadism as black slaves on plantations endured them – here presented as titillatory. The limericks followed almost weakly on from such a world exposed in all its horror. Their horrendous (and far from unusual) subject matter has a natural home here. The editor declares he will satisfy a long-felt want, often expressed, to supply material which 'the votaries of Venus' deserve, the devotees of 'the little blind god / who has no breeches on . . . ' Since they are 'determined to get from life the acme of enjoyment, the maximum of pleasure with the minimum of pain', they should regard this magazine as 'especially devoted to their interests'.

Legman makes a case for what happens in societies that repress sexuality in the way that Britain did, for example, in response to the dangers of the French Revolution. When moral wars are fought, they naturally lead to the immediate creation of a subterranean erotic folklore and literature. Joan Smith in her book *Mysogynies*, writing in 1989, more broadly tackles the thesis that there is a hidden passion that always distorts human relations. Women-hating, she suggests in her chapter titled 'Crawling from the Wreckage', is part of the necessary armour of the male bomber pilot (and soldier/sailor and, *ergo*, most other men) who defends his country. Needing to reaffirm his masculine identity, he must separate himself from women and prize this absence of feeling. When men are 'suddenly caught unawares, whether by love or lust or pity or rage, they have no experience . . . to guide them . . . ' and having built up their defences, they cannot cope with the intense urges or desires which may lead to relaxed happiness and which may become a threat to their carefully constructed masculine existence. They enshrine this position in their vocabulary and in the songs of barrackroom and bar. Society accepts and gives support to this. Its literature addresses this tension; some literary forms will debate it and others embrace it. The limerick effortlessly does the latter.

Following the gentle beginnings of Lear's wildly nonsensical verse, you will thus find placed the obscene and the indecent. Some people think that to work properly, the limerick must be sexist or racist, it must be offensive in some way for the fifth line to impact. The canon cannot be broadly represented without its sexual side, works such as *Cythera's Hymnal, or Flakes from a Foreskin* and *The Pearl: A Monthly Journal of Facetiae and Voluptuous Reading* being seminal (*sic*). But I found it painless to discard those limericks which were pertinent to race where ethnicity took over from mere geography.

And 'the best limerick of all'? Langford Reed wrote to dozens of his correspondents in 1925, asking them to name their choice. He arrived at the conclusion that this was the most popular:

> There was a young lady of Riga,
> Who smiled as she rode on a tiger;
> They returned from the ride
> With the lady inside,
> And the smile on the face of the tiger.

or, if you are a classical scholar:

> Puella Rigensis ridebat
> Cum tigris in tergo sedebat
> Externo profecta
> Interno revecta
> Sed risus cum tigre manebat

Of course, it may not be your favourite limerick; indeed you may fail to find your favourite in this anthology. This may be because of copyright or libel considerations, but if you feel that there are serious omissions, please write to me c/o Wordsworth Editions Limited, 8B

East Street, Ware, Hertfordshire SG12 9HJ and I will consider them for inclusion in any reprints.

And finally I wish to acknowledge the help and suggestions given to me by Brother Christian, Philip Stuart and Conor McHugh; without them this collection would never have been completed

LINDA MARSH

Gentle Beginnings *

❦

I

There was an old woman of Lynn,
Whose nose very near reach'd her chin;
    You may easy suppose
    She had plenty of beaux,
This charming old woman of Lynn.

The History of Sixteen Wonderful
Old Women (1820), AUTHOR UNKNOWN

2

There was an old woman of Gloster,
Whose parrot two guineas it cost her;
    But his tongue never ceasing,
    Was vastly displeasing,
To that talkative woman of Gloster.

The History of Sixteen Wonderful
Old Women (1820), AUTHOR UNKNOWN

3

There was a sick man of Tobago,
Lived long on rice-gruel and sago;
    But at last, to his bliss,
    The physician said this:
'To a roast leg of mutton you may go.'

Anecdotes and Adventures of Fifteen
Gentlemen (1822), AUTHOR UNKNOWN

* Unless attributed to another, all the limericks in this section are by Edward Lear
and are illustrated with his own drawings.

4

There was an old miser of Reading,
Had a house, with a yard, with a shed in;
   'Twas meant for a cow,
   But so small that I vow
The poor creature could scarce get its head in.

*Anecdotes and Adventures of Fifteen
Gentlemen (1822)*, AUTHOR UNKNOWN

5

There was a young person in pink,
Who called out for something to drink;
   But they said, 'O my daughter,
   There's nothing but water!'
Which vexed that young person in pink.

6

There was an old person of Sheen,
Whose expression was calm and serene;
   He sat in the water,
   And drank bottled porter,
That placid old person of Sheen.

7

There was an old person of Florence,
Who held mutton chops in abhorrence;
    He purchased a bustard,
    And fried him in mustard,
Which choked that old person of Florence.

8

There was an old person of Loo,
Who said, 'What on earth shall I do?'
    When they said, 'Go away!'
    She continued to stay,
That vexatious old person of Loo.

9

There was an old man of Spithead,
Who opened the window and said –
    'Fil-jomble, fil-jumble,
    Fil-rumble-come-tumble!'
That doubtful old man of Spithead.

10

There was an old person of Brigg,
Who purchased no end of a Wig;
 So that only his nose
 And the end of his toes
Could be seen when he walked about Brigg.

11

There was an old person of Deal,
Who in walking used only his heel;
 When they said, 'Tell us why?'
 He made no reply;
That mysterious old person of Deal.

12

There was an old man of Thermopylae,
Who never did anything properly;
    But they said, 'If you choose
    To boil eggs in your shoes,
You shall never remain in Thermopylae.'

13

There was an old person of Crowle,
Who lived in the nest of an owl;
    When they screamed in the nest,
    He screamed out with the rest,
That depressing old person of Crowle.

14

There was an old person of Sestri,
Who sat himself down in the vestry;
    When they said, 'You are wrong!'
    He merely said, 'Bong!'
That repulsive old person of Sestri.

15

There was an old person in grey,
Whose feelings were tinged with dismay;
    She purchased two parrots
    And fed them with carrots,
Which pleased that old person in grey.

16

There was an old person of Bow,
Whom nobody happened to know;
    So they gave him some soap,
    And said coldly, 'We hope
You will go back directly to Bow!'

17

There was an old person of Bude,
Whose deportment was vicious and crude;
    He wore a large ruff
    Of pale straw-coloured stuff,
Which perplexed all the people of Bude.

18

There was an old man in a tree,
Whose Whiskers were lovely to see;
    But the birds of the air
    Pluck'd them perfectly bare,
To make themselves nests in that tree.

19

There was a young lady of Corsica,
Who purchased a little brown saucy-cur;
    Which she fed upon ham
    And hot raspberry jam,
That expensive young lady of Corsica.

20

There was an old person of Skye,
Who waltz'd with a bluebottle fly;
    They buzz'd a sweet tune,
    To the light of the moon,
And entranced all the people of Skye.

21

There was an old man of Dunblane,
Who greatly resembled a crane;
    But they said – 'Is it wrong,
    Since your legs are so long,
To request you won't stay in Dunblane?'

22

There was an old person of Ware,
Who rode on the back of a bear;
     When they ask'd, 'Does it trot?'
     He said, 'Certainly not!
He's a Moppsikon Floppsikon bear!'

23

There was an old man of Dumbree,
Who taught little owls to drink tea;
     For he said, 'To eat mice
     Is not proper or nice,'
That amiable man of Dumbree.

24

There was an old person of Shoreham,
Whose habits were marked by decorum;
    He bought an umbrella,
    And sat in the cellar,
Which pleased all the people of Shoreham.

25

There was an old person of Wilts,
Who constantly walked upon stilts;
    He wreathed them with lilies
    And daffy-down-dillies,
That elegant person of Wilts.

26

There was an old man whose remorse,
Induced him to drink caper sauce;
    For they said, 'If mixed up
    With some cold claret-cup,
It will certainly soothe your remorse!'

27

There was an old person of Filey,
Of whom his acquaintance spoke highly;
    He danced perfectly well
    To the sound of a bell,
And delighted the people of Filey.

28

There was an old man of El Hums,
Who lived upon nothing but crumbs
    Which he picked off the ground,
    With the other birds round,
In the roads and the lanes of El Hums.

29

There was an old man of Messina,
Whose daughter was named Opsibeena;
    She wore a small wig
    And rode out on a pig,
To the perfect delight of Messina.

30

There was a young lady whose nose
Continually prospers and grows;
    When it grew out of sight,
    She exclaimed in a fright,
'Oh! Farewell to the end of my nose!'

31

There was an old lady of Winchelsea,
Who said, 'If you needle or pin shall see
    On the floor of my room,
    Sweep it up with the broom!'
That exhaustive old lady of Winchelsea!

32

There was an old man, who when little
Fell casually into a kettle;
 But, growing too stout,
  He could never get out,
So he passed all his life in that kettle.

33

There was a young lady in white,
Who looked out at the depths of the night;
 But the birds of the air,
  Filled her heart with despair,
And oppressed that young lady in white.

34

There was an old person of Putney,
Whose food was roast spiders and chutney,
    Which he took with his tea,
    Within sight of the sea,
That romantic old person of Putney.

35

There was an old man on whose nose
Most birds of the air could repose;
    But they all flew away
    At the closing of day,
Which relieved that old man and his nose.

36

There was a young lady of Clare,
Who was sadly pursued by a bear;
    When she found she was tired,
    She abruptly expired,
That unfortunate lady of Clare.

37

There was a young lady of Parma,
Whose conduct grew calmer and calmer;
    When they said, 'Are you dumb?'
    She merely said, 'Hum!'
That provoking young lady of Parma.

38

There was an old man who said, 'How
Shall I flee from that horrible cow?
    I will sit on this stile,
    And continue to smile,
Which may soften the heart of that cow.'

39

There was an old man of Aosta,
Who possessed a large cow, but he lost her;
    But they said, 'Don't you see,
    She has rushed up a tree?
You invidious old man of Aosta!'

40

There was an old person of Ems,
Who casually fell in the Thames;
    And when he was found,
    They said he was drowned,
That unlucky old person of Ems.

41

There was an old person of Ewell,
Who chiefly subsisted on gruel;
    But to make it more nice
    He inserted some mice,
Which refreshed that old person of Ewell.

42

There was an old lady of Prague,
Whose language was horribly vague;
 When they said, 'Are these caps?'
 She answered, 'Perhaps!'
That oracular lady of Prague.

43

There was an old person of Sparta,
Who had twenty-five sons and one 'darter';
 He fed them on snails,
 And weighed them in scales,
That wonderful person of Sparta.

44

There was an old person of Gretna,
Who rushed down the crater of Etna;
    When they said, 'Is it hot?'
    He replied, 'No, it's not!'
That mendacious old person of Gretna.

45

There was a young lady of Sweden,
Who went by the slow train to Weedon;
    When they cried, 'Weedon Station!'
    She made no observation
But thought she should go back to Sweden.

46

There was an old man of the Cape,
Who possessed a large Barbary ape,
    Till the ape one dark night
    Set the house all alight,
Which burned that old man of the Cape.

47

There was a young girl of Majorca,
Whose aunt was a very fast walker;
    She walked seventy miles,
    And leaped fifteen stiles,
Which astonished that girl of Majorca.

48

There was a young lady of Welling,
Whose praise all the world was a-telling;
 She played on a harp,
 And caught several carp,
That accomplished young lady of Welling.

49

There was an old person of Tartary,
Who divided his jugular artery;
 But he screeched to his wife,
 And she said, 'Oh, my life!
Your death will be felt by all Tartary!'

50

There was an old person of Spain,
Who hated all trouble and pain;
    So he sat on a chair,
    With his feet in the air,
That umbrageous old person of Spain.

51

There was an old man of the coast,
Who placidly sat on a post;
    But when it was cold
    He relinquished his hold
And called for some hot buttered toast.

52

There was an old man of Berlin,
Whose form was uncommonly thin;
    Till he once, by mistake,
    Was mixed up in a cake,
So they baked that old man of Berlin.

53

There was a young lady of Tyre,
Who swept the loud chords of a lyre;
    At the sound of each sweep
    She enraptured the deep,
And enchanted the city of Tyre.

54

There was an old person of Bangor,
Whose face was distorted with anger!
    He tore off his boots,
    And subsisted on roots,
That irascible person of Bangor.

55

There was an old man who said, 'Hush!
I perceive a young bird in this bush!'
    When they said, 'Is it small?'
    He replied, 'Not at all!
It is four times as big as the bush!'

56

There was an old man in a pew,
Whose waistcoat was spotted with blue;
    But he tore it in pieces
    To give to his nieces,
That cheerful old man in a pew.

57

There was an old person of Troy,
Whose drink was warm brandy and soy,
    Which he took with a spoon,
    By the light of the moon,
In sight of the city of Troy.

58

There was an old person of Cromer,
Who stood on one leg to read Homer;
    When he found he grew stiff,
    He jumped over the cliff,
Which concluded that person of Cromer.

59

There was an old person of Rheims,
Who was troubled with horrible dreams;
    So, to keep him awake,
    They fed him with cake,
Which amused that old person of Rheims.

60

There was an old man of the Nile,
Who sharpened his nails with a file,
　　Till he cut off his thumbs,
　　And said calmly, 'This comes
Of sharpening one's nails with a file!'

61

There was an old lady whose folly
Induced her to sit in a holly;
　　Whereupon, by a thorn
　　Her dress being torn,
She quickly became melancholy.

62

There was an old man of Nepal,
From his horse had a terrible fall;
    But, though split quite in two,
    With some very strong glue
They mended that man of Nepal.

63

There was an old man of th' Abruzzi,
So blind that he couldn't his foot see;
    When they said, 'That's your toe!'
    He replied, 'Is it so?'
That doubtful old man of th' Abruzzi.

64

There was an old man of Apulia,
Whose conduct was very peculiar:
 He fed twenty sons
 Upon nothing but buns,
That whimsical man of Apulia.

65

There was an old man with a poker,
Who painted his face with red ochre;
 When they said, 'You're a Guy!'
 He made no reply,
But knocked them all down with his poker.

66

There was a young lady whose nose
Was so long that it reached to her toes;
    So she hired an old lady,
    Whose conduct was steady,
To carry that wonderful nose.

67

There was a young lady of Turkey,
Who wept when the weather was murky;
    When the day turned out fine,
    She ceased to repine,
That capricious young lady of Turkey.

68

There was an old person whose habits
Induced him to feed upon rabbits;
    When he'd eaten eighteen,
    He turned perfectly green,
Upon which he relinquished those habits.

69

There was an old person of Dover,
Who rushed through a field of blue clover;
    But some very large bees
    Stung his nose and his knees,
So he very soon went back to Dover.

70

There was an old man of the Wrekin,
Whose shoes made a horrible creaking;
   But they said, 'Tell us whether
   Your shoes are of leather,
Or of what, you old man of the Wrekin?'

71

There was a young lady of Ryde,
Whose shoe-strings were seldom untied.
   She purchased some clogs,
   And some small spotted dogs,
And frequently walked about Ryde.

72

There was an old lady of Chertsey,
Who made a remarkable curtsey;
    She twirled round and round
    Till she sank underground,
Which distressed all the people of Chertsey.

73

There was an old man of the Dee,
Who was sadly annoyed by a flea;
    When he said, 'I will scratch it,'
    They gave him a hatchet,
Which grieved that old man of the Dee.

74

There was an old man of Vienna,
Who lived upon tincture of senna;
    When that did not agree,
    He took camomile tea,
That nasty old man of Vienna.

75

There was a young lady whose eyes
Were unique as to colour and size;
    When she opened them wide,
    People all turned aside,
And started away in surprise.

76

There was an old man with a beard,
Who said, 'It is just as I feared! –
    Two owls and a hen,
    Four larks and a wren,
Have all built their nests in my beard!'

77

There was an old person of Dean,
Who dined on one pea and one bean;
    For he said, 'More than that
    Would make me too fat,'
That cautious old person of Dean.

78

There was a young person whose history
Was always considered a mystery;
    She sat in a ditch,
    Although no one knew which,
And composed a small treatise on history.

79

There was an old man of Cape Horn,
Who wished he had never been born;
    So he sat on a chair,
    Till he died of despair,
That dolorous man of Cape Horn.

80

There was a young man of Cape Horn
Who wished he had never been born;
   And he wouldn't have been
   If his father had seen
That the end of the rubber was torn.

attributed to ALGERNON CHARLES SWINBURNE (1837–1909)

81

There was an old man of Dundee,
Who frequented the top of a tree;
   When disturbed by the crows,
   He abruptly arose,
And exclaimed, 'I'll return to Dundee.'

82

There was an old man of Dundee
Who molested an ape in a tree:
   The result was most horrid,
   All arse and no forehead,
Three balls and a purple goatee.

attributed to ALGERNON CHARLES SWINBURNE

83

There was a young lady of Norway,
Who casually sat in a doorway;
　　When the door squeezed her flat,
　　She exclaimed, 'What of that?'
This courageous young lady of Norway.

84

There was a young lady of Norway
Who hung by her toes in a doorway.
　　She said to her beau:
　　'Just look at me, Joe,
I think I've discovered one more way.'

attributed to ALGERNON CHARLES SWINBURNE

85

There was a young lady of Greenwich,
Whose garments were border'd with spinach;
    But a large spotty calf
    Bit her Shawl quite in half,
Which alarmed that young lady of Greenwich.

86

There once was a young man of Greenwich
Whose balls were all covered with spinach;
    So long was his tool
    That it wound round a spool
And he let it out inach by inach.

attributed to ALGERNON CHARLES SWINBURNE

87

There was an old man in a Tree,
Who was horribly bored by a bee;
    When they said, 'Does it buzz?'
    He replied, 'Yes, it does!
It's a regular brute of a bee!'

88

There was an old man of St Bees
Who was strung in the arm by a wasp.
    When they asked, 'Does it hurt?'
    He replied, 'No, it doesn't!
But I thought all the while 'twas a hornet.'

W. S. GILBERT (1836–1911)

89

I shall, with cultured taste,
Distinguish gems from paste,
    And 'High diddle diddle'
    Will rank as an idyll
If I pronounce it chaste!   W. S. GILBERT

90

Oh, my name is John Wellington Wells,
I'm a dealer in magic and spells,
    In blessings and curses,
    And ever-filled purses,
    In prophecies, witches and knells.   W. S. GILBERT

91

Of Agib, who amid Tartaric scenes,
Wrote a lot of ballet music in his teens;
    His gentle spirit rolls
    In the melody of souls –
Which is pretty, but I don't know what it means.

W. S. GILBERT

92

There was a professor named Chesterton,
Who went for a walk with his best shirt on.
    Being hungry, he ate it,
    But lived to regret it,
And ruined his life for his digestion.   W. S. GILBERT

93

If you want a proud foe to 'make tracks' –
If you'd melt a rich uncle in wax –
    You've but to look in
    On our resident djinn,
Number seventy, Simmery Axe . . .   W. S. GILBERT

94

There is a creator named God
Whose doings are sometimes quite odd.
    He made a painter named Val,
    And I say – and I shall –
That he does no credit to God.

JAMES ABBOTT MCNEIL WHISTLER (1834–1903)

95

The Reverend Henry Ward Beecher
Called a hen a most elegant creature.
    The hen, pleased with that,
    Laid an egg in his hat,
And thus did the hen reward Beecher.

OLIVER WENDALL HOLMES (1809–94)

96

A man hired by John Smith and Co.
Loudly declared that he'd tho.
   Men that he saw
   Dumping dirt by the door –
The drivers, therefore, didn't do.

MARK TWAIN (1835–1910)

97

There was a young girl of Aberystwyth
Who took grain to the mill to make grist with.
   The miller's son Jack,
   Laid her on her back,
And united the organs they pissed with.

ALGERNON CHARLES SWINBURNE

98

There was a young lady of Limerick
Who stole from a farmer named Tim a rick;
   When the priest at the altar
   Suggested a halter,
She fled from the county of Limerick.

ANDREW LANG (1844–1912)

99

'Tis strange how the newspapers honour
A creature that's called prima donna.
   They say not a thing
   Of how she can sing
But reams of the clothes she has on her.

EUGENE FIELD (1850–1895)

100

Now what in the world shall we dioux
With the bloody and murderous Sioux,
   Who some time ago
   Took an arrow and bow
And raised such a hellabelioux?

EUGENE FIELD

101

There is an old he-wolf named Gambart,
Beware of him if thou a lamb art;
   Else thy tail and thy toes,
   And thy innocent nose,
Will be ground by the grinder of Gambart.

DANTE GABRIEL ROSSETTI (1828–82)

102

There is a creature called God,
Whose creations are some of them odd.
   I maintain, and I shall,
   The creation of Val
Reflects little credit on God.   DANTE GABRIEL ROSSETTI

103

There's a combative artist named Whistler
Who is, like his own hog-hairs, a bristler;
   A tube of white lead
   And a punch on the head
Offer varied attractions to Whistler.

DANTE GABRIEL ROSSETTI

104

There's a Portuguese person named Howell
Who lays on his lies with a trowel;
   Should he give over lying,
   'Twill be when he's dying,
For living is lying with Howell.   DANTE GABRIEL ROSSETTI

105

There once was a painter named Scott.
Who seemed to have hair but had not.
   He seemed to have sense,
   'Twas an equal pretence
On the part of the painter named Scott.

DANTE GABRIEL ROSSETTI

106

There's an Irishman, Arthur O' Shaughnessy –
On the chessboard of poets a pawn is he;
    Though a bishop or king
    Would be rather the thing
To the fancy of Arthur O'Shaughnessy.

DANTE GABRIEL ROSSETTI

107

There is a big artist named Val,
The roughs' and the prize-fighters' pal.
    The mind of a groom
    And the head of a broom
Were Nature's endowments to Val.   D. G. ROSSETTI

108

There's a publishing party named Ellis,
Who's addicted to poets with bellies.
    He has at least two –
    One in fact, one in view –
And God knows what will happen to Ellis.

D. G. ROSSETTI

109

There is a poor sneak called Rossetti,
As a painter with many kicks met he –
    With more as a man –
    But sometimes he ran,
And that saved the rear of Rossetti.   D. G. ROSSETTI

110

There was an old man of the Cape
Who made himself garments of crêpe;
    When asked, 'Do they tear?'
    He replied, 'Here and there;
But they're perfectly splendid for shape.'

ROBERT LOUIS STEVENSON (1850–94)

111

There was a young woman of Aenos
Who came to our party as Venus.
  We told her how rude
  'Twas to come there quite nude,
And we brought her a leaf from the green-h'us.

THOMAS BAILEY ALDRICH (1836–1907)

112

There was a young lady of station,
'I love man' was her exclamation;
  But when men cried: 'You flatter!'
  She replied: 'Oh, no matter!'
'Isle of Man' is the explanation.

LEWIS CARROLL (REVD CHARLES
LUTWIDGE DODGSON) (1832–98)

113

There was once a young man of Oporto
Who daily got shorter and shorter;
  The reason he said
  Was the hod on his head,
Which was filled with the heaviest mortar.

LEWIS CARROLL

114

His sister, called Lucy O'Finner,
Grew constantly thinner and thinner;
  The reason was plain –
  She slept out in the rain,
And was never allowed any dinner.   LEWIS CARROLL

115

There was a young lady of Whitby,
Who had the bad luck to be bit by
  Two brown little things
  Without any wings,
And now she's uncomfy to sit by.   LEWIS CARROLL

116

There was a young genius of Queen's,
Who was fond of exploding machines.
   He once blew up a door,
   But he'll do it no more,
For it chanced that the door was the Dean's.

ARTHUR CLEMENT HILTON (1851–77)

117

There was an old Fellow of Trinity,
A doctor well versed in Divinity,
   But he took to free thinking,
   And then to deep drinking,
And so had to leave the vicinity.

ARTHUR CLEMENT HILTON

118

There was a young critic of King's,
Who had views on the limits of things.
With the size of his chapel,
He would frequently grapple,
And exclaim: 'It is biggish for King's.'

ARTHUR CLEMENT HILTON

119

There was a young gourmand of John's,
Who'd a notion of dining on swans.
   To the Backs he took big nets
   To capture the cygnets,
But was told they were kept for the dons.

ARTHUR CLEMENT HILTON

Perkins and his Gherkins
Limericks for the Respectable

❧

1

There once was a plesiosaurus,
Who lived when the world was all porous;
 But it fainted with shame,
 When it first heard its name,
And departed long ages before us.

2

A traveller to Timbuktu
Said: 'Pilot! It's time that we flew!'
 He replied: 'That will do!
 Your watch is askew:
It's a minute or two to 2.02.'

3

A wonderful fish is the flea,
He bores and he bites on me.
 I would love, indeed,
 To watch him feed,
But he bites me where I cannot see.

4

An amoeba, named Sam, and his brother
Were having a drink with each other;
 In the midst of their quaffing,
 They split themselves laughing,
And each of them now is a mother.

5

There was an old man of Blackheath,
Who sat on his set of false teeth.
 Said he with a start,
 'Oh Lor, bless my heart!
I have bitten myself underneath!'

6

There was a young lady from Coleshill,
Who incautiously sat on a mole's hill.
 An inquisitive mole
 Poked his nose up her hole.
The gal's OK but the mole's ill.

7

As a beauty, I'm not a star,
There are many more handsome by far;
 But my face, I don't mind it,
 For I am behind it,
It's the people in front get the jar.

8

A knight in a chapel in Ealing,
Who had spent several centuries kneeling,
 Said, 'Please keep off my arse
 When you're rubbing my brass:
It gives me a very strange feeling.'

9

A short-sighted man from Havana
Confused clothing with flora and fauna;
 He was heard to say 'Ouch'
 When a black posing pouch
Turned out to be three small piranha.

10

I once thought a lot of a friend
Who turned out to be in the end
   The southernmost part
   (As I'd feared from the start)
Of a horse with a northerly trend.

11

A newspaper writer named Fling
Could make copy from most anything;
   But the copy he wrote
   Of a ten-dollar note
Was so good he is now in Sing Sing.

12

There was a young lady of Crewe
Who wanted to catch the 2:02.
   Said a porter, 'Don't worry,
   Or hurry, or scurry,
It's a minute or two to 2:02.'

13

A menagerie came to Cape Race
Where they loved the gorilla's grimace.
   It surprised them to learn
   That he *owned* the concern:
He was human, in spite of his face!

14

In Boston a sub-deb named Brooks
Had a hobby of reading sex books.
   She married a Cabot
   Who looked like a rabbit
And deftly lived up to his looks.

15

The thoughts of the rabbit on sex
Are seldom, if ever, complex;
   For a rabbit in need
   Is a rabbit indeed,
And does just as a person expects.

16

'I shall star,' vowed a girl from Biloxi,
'At Twentieth-Century-Foxi,'
   And her movie career
   Really prospered last year:
She's in charge of the mops at the Roxi.

17

A drunken old tar from St Clements,
To ward off the scurvy sucked lemons.
   'With my health unimpaired
   I'll have time,' he declared,
'To die of delirium tremens.'

18

A discerning person from Swaffham
Would seek out real ales, and then quaff 'em;
   The problem that played
   On the mind of the trade
Lay in getting the cost of them off him.

19

There was a young man so benighted,
He never knew when he was slighted.
   He went to a party,
   And ate just as hearty
As if he'd been really invited.

20

There was a co-ed of Cayenne
Who ate onions, blue cheese and sen-sen.
  Till a bad fright one day
  Took her breath quite away,
And we hope she won't find it again.

21

There was a young lady of Herm
Who tied bows on the tail of a worm.
  Said she, 'You look festive,
  But don't become restive;
You'll wriggle them off if you squirm.'

22

An unfortunate dumb mute from Kew
Was trying out signs that he knew.
  He did them so fast
  That his fingers at last
Got so tangled he fractured a few.

23

Some amateur players, most brave,
A performance of *Hamlet* once gave.
  Said a wag, 'Now let's see
  If it's Bacon or he –
I mean Shakespeare – who's turned in his grave.'

24

There once was a curate of Kew
Who kept a tom-cat in a pew.
  He taught it to speak
  Alphabetical Greek
But it never got further than μ.

25

Miss Vera de Peyster Depew
Disdained anything that was new.
   She said, 'I do not
   Know exactly what's what
But I know without question Who's Who.'

26

Two beauties who dwelt by the Bosphorus
Had eyes that were brighter than phosphorous.
   The sultan cried, 'Troth!
   I'd marry you both!'
But they laughed, 'I'm afraid you must toss for us.'

27

An important young man from Quebec
Had to welcome the Duchess of Teck,
   So he bought for a dollar
   A very high collar
To save himself washing his neck.

28

There was an old widower, Doyle,
Who wrapped up his wife in tin foil.
   He thought it would please her
   To stay in the freezer
And anyway, outside she'd spoil.

29

There was an old fellow from Croydon,
Whose cook was a cute little hoyden.
   She would sit on his knees
   While shelling the peas
Or pleasanter duties employed on.

30

Rebecca, a silly young wench,
Went out on the Thames to catch tench.
　　When the boat was upset,
　　She exclaimed, I regret,
A five-letter word – and in French!

31

There was an old maid of Genoa,
And I blush when I think what Iowa.
　　She's gone to her rest,
　　And it's all for the best,
Otherwise I would borrow Samoa.

32

An oyster from Kalamazoo
Confessed he was feeling quite blue.
　　For he said, 'As a rule,
　　When the weather turns cool,
I invariably get in a stew.'

33

To his wife said a grumbler named Dutton,
'I'm a gourmet, I am, not a glutton
　　For ham, jam or lamb
　　I don't give a damn,
So come on, let's return to our mutton.'

34

Said a foolish householder of Wales,
'An odour of coal gas prevails.'
　　She then struck a light
　　And later that night
Was collected in seventeen pails.

35

There was a young man at the War Office
Whose brain was as good as a store office.
  Every warning severe
  Simply went in one ear
And out of the opposite orifice.

36

There was a good canon of Durham
Who fished with a hook and a worrum.
  Said the dean to the bishop,
  'I've brought a big fish up,
But I fear we will have to inter'm.'

37

There was an old lady of Rye,
Who was baked by mistake in a pie.
  To the householder's disgust
  She emerged in the crust
And exclaimed with a yawn, 'Where am I?'

38

A cannibal bold of Penzance
Ate an uncle and two of his aunts,
  A cow and her calf,
  An ox and a half,
And now he can't button his pants.

39

An eccentric old person of Slough,
Who took all of his meals with a cow,
  Always said, 'It's uncanny,
  She's so like Aunt Fanny,'
But he never would indicate how.

40

There was an old lady of Brooking,
Who had a great genius for cooking.
   She could bake sixty pies,
   All quite the same size,
And tell which was which without looking.

41

A visitor once to Loch Ness
Met the monster, who left him a mess;
   They returned his entrails
   By the regular mails
And the rest of the stuff by express.

42

There's a lady in Kalamazoo
Who first bites her oysters in two;
   She has a misgiving,
   Should any be living,
They'd raise such a hullabaloo.

43

There once was a damsel named Jinx,
Who when asked what she thought of the Sphinx,
   Replied with a smile,
   'That old fraud by the Nile?
I personally think that she stinks.'

44

An eccentric old spinster named Lowell
Announced to her friends, 'Bless my sowell,
   I've gained so much weight,
   I am sorry to state,
I fear that I'm going to fowell.'

45

As they fished his old plane from the sea.
The inventor just chortled with glee.
   'I shall build,' and he laughed,
   'A submarine craft,
And perhaps it will fly, we shall see.'

46

There was a young charmer named Sheba,
Whose pet was a darling amoeba.
   This queer blob of jelly
   Would lie on her belly
And blissfully murmer, 'Ich liebe.'

47

There was a young woman of Glasgow,
Whose party proved quite a fiasco.
   At 9.30, about,
   The lights all went out,
Through a lapse on the part of the Gas Co.

48

There was a young person from Perth
Who was born on the day of his birth.
   He was married, they say,
   On his wife's wedding day,
And died when he quitted this earth.

49

There was a young curate of Minster,
Who admonished a giddy young spinster.
   For she used, on the ice,
   Words not at all nice
When he, at a turn, slid against her.

50

There was a young parson, called Perkins,
Exceedingly fond of small gherkins.
　　One summer at tea
　　He ate forty-three,
Which pickled his internal workins.

51

There was an old cadger of Broome,
Who kept a baboon in his room.
　　'It reminds me,' he said,
　　'Of a friend who is dead.'
But he never would tell us of whom.

52

Our vicar is good Mr Inge.
One evening he offered to sing.
　　So we asked him to stoop,
　　Put his head in a loop,
And pulled at each end of the string.

53

There was a young lady of Ryde
Whose locks were considerably dyed
　　The hue of her hair
　　Made everyone stare:
'She's piebald, she'll die bald!' they cried.

54

A cynic of much *savoir-faire*
Pursued by a horrible bear,
　　Said, 'I'll argue a while
　　In the feminine style.
No creature could follow me there.'

55

There was an old lady of Tooting
Who wanted to learn parachuting.
  Though they tried to repress her,
  She jumped from the dresser,
A perfect vol-plane executing.

56

The bishop of Ibu Plantation
Wrote a thesis on transfiguration
  For the *Christian Review*
  (As all good bishops do)
While practising miscegenation.

57

There was a young maid who said, 'Why
Can't I look in my ear with my eye?
  If I give my mind to it,
  I'm sure I can do it
You never can tell till you try.'

58

A classical scholar from Flint
Developed a curious squint.
  With her left-handed eye
  She could scan the whole sky
While the other was reading small print.

59

There once was a boy from Baghdad,
An inquisitive sort of a lad.
  He said, 'Let us see
  If a sting has a bee,'
And he very soon found that it had.

60

The conquering Lion of Judah
Made a prayer to the statue of Buddha.
'O Idol,' he prayed,
'May Il Duce be spayed,
And all his descendants be neuter!'

61

There was a young lady of Wilts,
Who walked to the Highlands on stilts.
 When they said, 'Oh, how shocking,
 To show so much stocking!'
She answered, 'Well, how about kilts?'

62

They say that I was, in my youth,
Uncouth and ungainly, forsooth;
 I can only reply:
 ' 'Tis a lie, 'tis a lie!
I was couth, I was perfectly couth!'

63

There was a brave damsel of Brighton
Whom nothing could possibly frighten.
 She plunged in the sea
 And, with infinite glee,
Sailed away on the back of a triton.

64

Said a logical linguist named Rolles,
'As we always call Polish folk "Poles",
 For better precision
 (I am a logician)
We ought to call Dutch people "Holes".'

65

There was a young lady of Venice
Who used hard-boiled eggs to play tennis.
  People said, 'That is wrong.'
  She replied, 'Go along!
You don't know how prolific my hen is.'

66

There was a young girl of West Ham
Who hastily jumped on a tram.
  When she had embarked
  The conductor remarked,
'Your fare, miss.' She answered, 'I am.'

67

A society climber from Crewe
Enquired, 'What on earth shall I do?
  I of course know what's what,
  But I fear I have not
The faintest idea of who's who.'

68

There was a young poet of Kew
Who failed to emerge into view;
  So he said, 'I'll dispense
  With rhyme, metre and sense.'
And he did; and he's now in *Who's Who*.

69

There was an old lady of Kent,
Whose nose was remarkably bent.
  One day, they suppose,
  She followed her nose,
For no one knew which way she went.

70

The village was giddy with rumours
Of a goat who was suffering from tumours.
  Cans and library paste
  Were quite to her taste
But she choked on Elizabeth's bloomers.

71

The mouth of a glutton named Moto
Was the size that no organ should grow to.
  It could take in with ease
  Six carrots, ten peas,
And a whole baked potato *in toto*.

72

There was an old skinflint named Green,
Who grew so abnormally lean
  And flat and compressed
  That his back squeezed his chest,
And sideways he couldn't be seen.

73

A housewife called out with a frown,
When surprised by some callers from town:
  'In a minute or less
  I'll slip on a dress – '
But she slipped on the stairs and fell down.

74

There was a young lady of Kent
Who always said just what she meant.
  People said, 'She's a dear –
  So unique – so sincere – '
But they shunned her by common consent.

75

There was a young lady of Crete,
Who was so exceedingly neat:
　　When she got out of bed
　　She stood on her head
To make sure of not soiling her feet.

76

There was a young man who was bitten
By twenty-two cats and a kitten.
　　Cried he, 'It is clear
　　My end is quite near!
No matter. I'll die like a Briton.'

77

There was an old woman of Clewer
Who was riding a bike, and it threw her.
　　A butcher came by
　　And said, 'Missus, don't cry,'
And fixed her back on, with a skewer.

78

An unfortunate lady named Piles
Had the ugliest bottom for miles;
　　But her surgeon took pity
　　And made it quite pretty:
All dimples, and poutings, and smiles.

79

When Daddy and Mum got quite plastered,
And their shame had been thoroughly mastered,
　　They told their boy Harry,
　　'Son, we never did marry;
But don't tell the neighbours, you bastard.'

80

A slumbering infant named Daniel
Dreamt his leg had been bit by a spaniel.
   He awoke from his dream
   With a blood-curdling scream.
Said the nurserymaid, 'My! that boy can yell.'

81

There was a dear lady of Eden,
Who on apples was quite fond of feedin'.
   She gave one to Adam,
   Who said, 'Thank you, Madam.'
And then both skedaddled from Eden.

82

There once was a girl from New York,
Whose body was lighter than cork;
   She had to be fed
   For six weeks upon lead
Before she went out for a walk.

83

There was an old man who said, 'Do
Tell me how I'm to add two and two.
   I'm not very sure
   That it doesn't make four,
But I fear that is almost too few.'

84

A Turk named Abdullah Ben Barum
Had sixty-five wives in his harem.
   When his favourite horse died,
   'Mighty Allah!' he cried.
'Take a few of my wives – I can spare 'em.'

85

There once was a pious young priest
Who lived almost wholly on yeast.
   'For,' he said, 'it is plain
   We must all rise again,
And I want to get started, at least.'

86

There once was a girl named O'Brien
Who taught holy hymns to a lion.
   Of the lady there's some
   In the lion's tum-tum;
The rest twangs a harp up in Zion.

87

There once was a man of Calcutta
Who spoke with a terrible stutter.
   At breakfast he said,
   'Give me some b–bread
And b–b–b–b–b–b–butter.'

88

A dentist named Archibald Moss
Fell in love with the toothsome Miss Ross,
   But he held in abhorrence
   Her Christian name, Florence,
So he renamed her his Dental Floss.

89

There was a great lord in Japan
Whose name on a Tuesday began;
   It carried through Sunday
   Till twilight on Monday,
And sounded like stones in a can.

90

A tiger, by taste anthropophagous,
Felt a yearning within his oesophagus;
   He spied a fat Brahmin
   And growled, 'What's the harm in
A peripatetic sarcophagus?'

91

A careless old cook of Saltash
With a second-hand car had a crash.
   She ploughed through a wall,
   House, garden and all,
And ended up banger and mash.

92

A tone-deaf old fellow of Tring,
When somebody asked him to sing,
   Replied, 'It is odd,
   But I cannot tell "God
Save the Weasel" from "Pop goes the King".'

93

There once was a bonnie Scotch laddie
Who said as he put on his plaidie,
   'I've just had a dish
   O' unco' guid fish.'
What had he had? Had he had haddie?

94

There was a young priest of Dun Laoghaire
Who stood on his head in the *Kyrie*;
   When people asked why,
   He said in reply:
'It's the latest liturgical theory.'

95

There was a young friar named Borrow
Who eloped with two nuns, to his sorrow.
    They lived on an isthmus,
    And one he named Christmas,
The other he christened Tomorrow.

96

A publisher went off to France,
In search of a tale of romance;
    A Parisian lady
    Told a story so shady
That the publisher made an advance.

97

A singer in Radio City
(Whose form is impressively pretty)
    Is often addressed
    By the name of 'Beau Chest',
Which is thought to be tasteful and witty.

98

A lady there was in Antigua
Who said to her spouse, 'What a pigua!'
    He answered, 'My queen,
    Is it my manners you mean,
Or do you refer to my figua?'

99

There was a young lady of Bandon
Whose feet were too narrow to stand on;
    So she stood on her head,
    'For my motto,' she said,
'Has always been *Nil desperandum*.'

100

Concerning the bees and the flowers,
In the fields and the gardens and bowers;
   You will tell at a glance
   That their ways of romance
Haven't any resemblance to ours.

101

There was a young fellow named Willie,
Who acted remarkably silly:
   At an All-Nations ball,
   Dressed in nothing at all,
He claimed that his costume was Chile.

102

Said the crow to a pelican, 'Grant
Me the loan of your bill; for my aunt
   Has asked me to tea.'
   Said the other, 'Not me:
Ask my brother – for this pelican't.'

103

A painter, who lived in Great Britain,
Interrupted two girls at their knitting.
   Said he, with a sigh,
   'That park bench, er – I
Just painted it right where you're sitting.'

104

There once was a sailor named Pink
Whose mates rushed him off to the clink.
   Said he: 'I've a skunk
   As a pet in my bunk –
That's no reason for raising a stink.'

105

There was an old justice, named Percival,
Who said, 'I suppose you'll get worse if I'll
    Send you to gaol,
    So I'll put you on bail.'
Now wasn't Judge Percival merciful?

106

There was a young man of Westphalia
Who yearly got tail-ier and tail-ier,
    Till he took on the shape
    Of a Barbary ape
With the consequent paraphernalia.

107

There once was a baby of yore
Whose parents found it a bore
    And, being afraid
    It might be mislaid,
They stored it away in a drawer.

108

Despite her impressive physique,
Fatima was really quite meek;
    If a mouse showed its head
    She would jump into bed
With a terrible blood-curdling shreik.

109

A lady removing her scanties
Heard them crackle electrical chanties;
    Said her husband, 'My dear,
    I very much fear
You suffer from amps in your panties.'

110

A contemptuous matron in Shoreham
Behaved with extreme indecorum.
  She snapped a sarcastic
  And secret elastic
Throughout the community forum.

111

A Korean whose home was in Seoul
Had notions uncommonly droll;
  He'd get himself stewed
  And pose in the nude
On top of a telephone pole.

112

There once was a girl from Revere
So enormously large that, oh, dear!
  Once far out in the ocean
  Byrd raised a commotion
By planting our flag on her rear.

113

A singular fellow of Weston
Has near fifty feet of intestine;
  Though a signal success
  In the medical press,
It isn't much good for digestin'.

114

A minister up in Vermont
Keeps a goldfish alive in the font;
  When he dips the babes in
  It tickles their skin,
Which is all that the innocents want.

115

There was a young woman of Thrace
Whose nose spread all over her face.
   She had very few kisses:
   The reason for this is
There wasn't a suitable place.

116

From a tree hung a queer three-toed sloth,
Who to move was exceedingly wroth.
   But up in the tree
   He spied him a she
And combined the best features of both.

117

A Tory, once out in his motor,
Ran over a Labourite voter.
   'Thank goodness,' he cried,
   'He was on the wrong side.
So I don't blame myself one iota.'

118

A sleeper from the Amazon
Put nighties of his gra'mazon –
   The reason: That
   He was too fat
To get his own pajamazon.

119

A two-toothed old man of Arbroath
Gave vent to a terrible oath.
   When one tooth chanced to ache,
   By an awful mistake
The dentist extracted them both.

120

There was a young man from Tacoma
Whose breath had a whiskey aroma;
   So to alter the smell
   He swallowed Chanel
And went off in a heavenly coma.

121

A hapless church tenor was Horace
Whose skin was so terribly porous,
   Sometimes in the choir
   He'd start to perspire,
And nearly drown out the whole chorus.

122

There was a young lady named Grace
Who had eyes in a very odd place.
   She could sit on the hole
   Of a mouse or a mole
And stare the beast square in the face.

123

In Paris some visitors go
To see what no person should know.
   And then there are tourists,
   The purest of purists,
Who say it is quite *comme il faut*.

124

A God-fearing maiden from Goshen
Took a September-morn swim in the ocean;
   When a whirlpool appeared
   She rose up and cheered
And developed a rotary motion.

125

There was a young lady called Hopper,
Who came a society cropper.
　　She determined to go
　　to Bordeaux with her beau . . .
The rest of the story's improper.

126

Have you heard about Madame Lupescu,
Who came to Rumania's rescue?
　　It's a wonderful thing
　　To be under a king.
Is democracy better? I ask you!

127

There was a most finicky lass,
Who always wore panties of brass.
　　When they asked, 'Don't they chafe?'
　　She said, 'Yes, but I'm safe
from prickles and pins in the grass.'

128

There was a young man of Hong Kong,
Who invented a topical song.
　　It wasn't the words
　　That bothered the birds
But the horrible double ontong.

129

A French poodle espied in the hall
A pool that a damp gamp let fall,
　　And said, '*Ah, oui, oui!*
　　This time it's not me;
But I'm bound to be blamed for it all!'

130

An adventurous fun-loving polyp
Propositioned a cute little scallop,
   Down under the sea;
   'Nothing doing,' said she;
'By Triton – you think I'm a trollop?'

131

There was a young lady of Ealing,
Who walked up and down on the ceiling;
   She shouted: 'Oh, heck!
   I've broken my neck,
And it is a peculiar feeling.'

132

There was a young fellow of Ceuta
Who rode into church on his scooter;
   He knocked down the dean,
   And said: 'Sorry, old bean!
I ought to have sounded my hooter.'

133

There were three little owls in a wood,
Who sang hymns whenever they could.
   What the words were about
   One could never make out,
But one felt it was doing them good.

134

When Tommy first saw Colonel Peake
(Now, Tommy is five and can speak),
   He said, 'Auntie Rose,
   Does he put on his nose
The same stuff you paint on your cheek?'

135

There once were some learnèd MDs
Who captured some germs of disease
   And infected a train,
   Which, without causing pain,
Allowed one to catch it with ease.

136

There was a young maid of Madras
Possessed of a beautiful ass:
   It was not round and pink,
   As you possibly think,
But was grey, had long ears, and ate grass.

137

A dentist who lives in Duluth
Has wedded a widow named Ruth.
   She is so sentimental
   Concerning things dental,
She calls her dear second her 'twoth'.

138

There was a young lady of Ealing
Who had an irrational feeling
   That she was a fly;
   So she felt she should try
To walk upside down on the ceiling.

139

There was a young cashier of Calais
Whose accounts, when reviewed, wouldn't talais;
   Soon his chief smelt a rat:
   For he'd furnished a flat,
And was seen every night at the balais.

140

There was a young man from Darjeeling
Who got on a bus bound for Ealing.
   It said at the door,
   'Don't spit on the floor';
So he carefully spat on the ceiling.

141

There was a young lady of Rye,
With a shape like a capital I.
   When they told her she had,
   She learned how to pad –
Which shows just how figures call lie.

142

There was a young lady of Cheadle
Who sat down in church on a needle;
   Though deeply embedded,
   'Twas luckily threaded,
So she had it removed by the beadle.

143

An old Quaker person of Fratton
Would sit in the church with his hat on.
   'When I wake up,' he said,
   'With my hat on my head,
I'm sure that it hasn't been sat on.'

144

There was an old lady of Harrow
Who rode into church in a barrow.
   When she stuck in the aisle,
   Said she, with a smile,
'They build these 'ere churches too narrow.'

145

There was a young girl from St Paul
Wore a newspaper dress to a ball;
   But the dress caught on fire
   And burned her entire –
Front page, sporting section and all.

146

A charming old lady of Settle
For a hat, wore a bright copper kettle.
   When people derided
   She said, 'I've decided
To show all the neighbours my mettle.'

147

A thrifty young fellow of Shoreham
Made brown paper trousers and woreham.
   He looked nice and neat,
   Till he bent in the street
To pick up a coin; then he toreham.

148

A writer named Barbara Pym
Indulged in a personal whim:
   She'd wear a large bonnet
   When writing a sonnet
and a helmet when writing a hymn.

149

Said an eminent, erudite ermine:
'There's one thing I cannot determine:
   When a dame wears my coat
   She's a person of note;
When I wear it, I'm called only vermin.'

150

There was once a lady of Erskine
Who had a remarkably fair skin.
 When I said to her, 'Mabel,
 You look well in sable,'
She replied, 'I look best in my bearskin.'

151

There once was a corpulent carp,
Who wanted to play on the harp;
 But to his chagrin,
 So short was his fin,
He couldn't reach up to C sharp.

152

There was an old lady of Wales
Who lived upon mussels and snails.
 On growing a shell,
 She exclaimed, 'Just as well! –
It will save me in bonnets and veils.'

153

A remarkable figure has Myrtle:
A retractable tail like a turtle.
 But though she has never
 Been called cute or clever,
She annually proves to be fertile.

154

There was an old person of Prague
Who was suddenly seized with the ague.
 But they gave him some butter
 Which caused him to stutter
And cured that old person's plague.

155

The bottle of perfume that Willie sent
Was highly displeasing to Millicent.
 Her thanks were so cold
 They quarrelled I'm told
Through the silly scent Willie sent Millicent.

156

A Kentucky-bound author named Vaughan,
Whose style often savoured of scorn,
 Soon inscribed in his journals,
 'Here the corn's full of kernels,
And the colonels are all full of corn.'

157

There was a man in Atchison
Whose trousers had rough patchison;
 He found them great
 He'd often state
To strike his safety matchison.

158

A hen who resided in Reading
Attended a gentleman's wedding.
 As she walked up the aisle
 The guests had to smile
In spite of the tears they were shedding.

159

You will find by the banks of the Nile
The haunts of the great crocodile.
 He will welcome you in
 With an innocent grin
Which gives way to a satisfied smile.

160

At the zoo I remarked to an emu,
'I cannot pretend I esteem you;
   You're a greedy old bird
   And your walk is absurd;
And not even your feathers redeem you!'

161

The kings of Peru were the Incas,
Who were known far and wide as great drincas;
   They worshipped the sun,
   And had lots of fun,
But the peons all thought them great stincas.

162

There was a young Jap on a syndicate,
Who refused his opinions to vindicate;
   He stoutly denied
   That his statements implied
What they seemed on the surface to indicate.

163

A sensitive girl called O'Neill
Went on the fairground Big Wheel;
   When half-way around
   She looked down at the ground
It cost her a two-dollar meal.

164

There was a young lady of Spain
Who was terribly sick in a train –
   Not once, but again
   And again and again –
And again and again and again.

165

When twins came, their father, Dann Dunn,
Gave Edward as name to each son.
   When folks cried, 'Absurd!'
   He replied, 'Ain't you heard
That two Eds are better than one?'

166

There was a young lady of Harwich
Whose conduct was odd at her marwich.
   She proceeded on skates
   To the parish church gates
While her friends followed on in a carwich.

167

God's plan made a hopeful beginning,
But Man spoilt his chances by sinning;
   We trust that the story
   Will end in great glory,
But at present, the other side's winning.

168

There was a young woman named Frances
Who decided to better her chances
   By cleverly adding
   Appropriate padding
To enlarge all her protuberances.

169

There was a fat lady of Clyde,
Whose shoelaces once came untied.
   She feared that to bend
   Would display her rear end,
So she cried and she cried and she cried.

170

There was a fat man from Lahore,
The same shape behind as before.
   They did not know where
   To offer a chair,
So he had to sit down on the floor.

171

An impish young fellow named James
Had a passion for idiot games.
   He lighted the hair
   Of his lady's affair,
And laughed as she peed out the flames.

172

There was an old fellow of Tyre
Who constantly sat on the fire.
   When asked, 'Are you hot?'
   He said, 'Certainly not,
I'm James Winterbottom, Esquire.'

173

A certain young laddie named Robbie
Rode his steed back and forth in the lobby;
   When they told him, 'Indoors
   'Is no place for a horse,'
He replied, 'Well, you see, it's my hobby.'

174

Said the Duke to the Duchess of Avery
'Forgive me for breaking your reverie;
   You've been sitting on *Punch*
   Since long before lunch –
Might I have it, before it's unsavoury?'

175

There was a young woman named Sue
Who saw a strange beast in the zoo;
   When she asked, 'Is it old?'
   She firmly was told,
'No! Certainly not! It is gnu.'

176

There was a young lady of Zion
Looked round for a shoulder to cry on;
   So she married a spouse
   From a very old house
And started to cry on the scion.

177

Cried a slender young lady named Toni
With a bottom exceedingly bony,
   'I'll say this for my rump:
   Though it may not be plump,
It's my own, not a silicone phoney!'

178

I sat next to the Duchess at tea.
It was just as I feared it would be:
   Her rumblings abdominal
   Were simply phenomenal,
And everyone thought it was me!

179

There once was a lady named Harris
That nothing seemed apt to embarrass
   Till the bathsalts she shook
   In a tub that she took
Turned out to be plaster of Paris.

180

Said a fair-headed maiden of Klondike:
'Of you I'm exceedingly fond, Ike.
   To prove I adore you,
   I'll dye, darling, for you,
And be a brunette, not a blonde, Ike.'

181

A lady on climbing Mount Shasta
Complained as the mountain grew vaster,
   That it wasn't the climb
   Nor the dirt nor the grime
But the ice on her ass that harassed her.

182

A certain young lady named Hannah
Was caught in a flood in Montannah.
   As she floated away
   Her beau, so they say,
Accompanied her on the piannah.

183

There was a young farmer named Max
Who avoided the gasoline tax;
   It was simple, you see,
   For his Vespa burned pee
From his grandfather's herd of tame yaks.

184

A disgusting young man named McGill
Made his neighbours exceedingly ill
   When they learned of his habits
   Involving white rabbits
And a bird with a flexible bill.

185

There was an old man who said, 'Please,
Give me some of your Cotherstone cheese.
   I have smelt it for miles
   Coming over the stiles
To your charming farmhouse on the Tees.

186

A vessel has sailed from Chicago
With barrels of pork for a cargo;
   For Boston she's bound,
   Preceded, I've found,
By another with beans from near Fargo.

187

A bibulous chap from Duquesne
Drank a whole jeroboam of champagne.
   Said he, with a laugh
   As he quaffed the last quaff,
'I tried to get drunk, but in vain!'

188

A wonderful bird is the pelican
His bill can hold more than his belican.
   He can take in his beak
   Enough food for a week.
But nobody knows how the helican.

189

In the days of mild Jerry Ford,
Decorum and calm were restored;
   He did nothing hateful,
   For which we were grateful,
And terribly, terribly bored.

190

'What have I done?' said Christine:
'I've ruined the party machine.
  To lie in the nude
  Is not very rude,
But to lie in the House is obscene.'

191

There was an old man of Tarentum,
Who gnashed his false teeth till he bent 'em.
  When they asked him the cost
  Of what he had lost,
He replied, 'I can't say, I just rent 'em.'

192

There's a clever old miser who tries
Every method to e–con–omise.
  He said with a wink,
  'I save gallons of ink
By simply not dotting my eyes.'

193

There was a young dandy of Bute
Who sported a very loud suit.
  When told, 'It's too loud,'
  He archly said, 'How'd
I look in a suit that was mute?'

194

There was a young lady of Cheltenham
Put on tights just to see how she felt in 'em;
  But she said, with a shout,
  'If you don't pull me out,
I'm sure I shall jolly soon melt in 'em.'

195

A tea-swilling publisher, Gee,
When he has distant clients to see
    Always travels by plane,
    And if pressed to explain,
Says, 'I just love TWA tea.'

196

A buxom young typist, named Baynes,
At her work took particular pains.
    She was good at dictation
    And long explanation;
But she ran more to bosom than brains.

197

There was a young dancer of Ipswich
Who tooks most astonishing skips, which
    So delighted a miss
    She said, 'Give me a kiss!'
He replied, 'On the cheek, or the lips – which?'

198

There was an old lady who said,
When she found a thief under her bed,
    'So near to the floor,
    And so close to the door!
I'm afraid you'll catch cold in your head.'

199

A major, with wonderful force,
Called out in Hyde Park for a horse.
    All the flowers looked round,
    But not one could be found,
So he just rhododendron, of course.

200

A statesman who lived near the Isis
Remarked to his cook in a crisis:
   'This meat is so tough
   It is more than enough
To give a gas oven gastritis!'

201

'I must leave here,' said Lady de Vere,
'For these damp airs don't suit me, I fear.'
   Said her friend: 'Goodness me!
   If they don't agree
With your system, why eat pears, my dear?'

202

There was an old woman of Filey
Who valued old candle-ends highly.
   When no one was looking
   She'd use them for cooking –
'It's wicked to waste,' she said, dryly.

203

Well, if it's a sin to like Guinness,
Then that I admit's what my sin is.
   I like it with fizz,
   Or just as it is,
And it's much better for me than gin is.

204

A Turk by the name of Haroun
Ate whisky by means of a spoon.
   When someone asked, 'Why?'
   He gave this reply,
'To drink is forbidden, you loon!'

205

A glutton from Bingen-am-Rhein
Was asked at what hour he would dine.
 He replied, 'At eleven,
 At three, five and seven,
And eight; and a quarter to nine.'

206

A dancing girl came to St Gall,
With a mouth so exceedingly small,
 That she said, 'It would be
 Much more easy for me
To do without eating at all.'

207

There was a young lady of Lynn
Who was so uncommonly thin
 That when she essayed
 To drink lemonade
She slipped through the straw and fell in.

208

A horrible brat from Belgravia
Drove his parents to thoughts of Our Savia.
 'By Jesus,' they swore,
 'We can't stand much more
Of this sonofabitch's behavia!'

209

There once were three fellows from Gary,
Named Larry and Harry and Barry;
 Now Harry was bare
 As an egg or a pear,
But Larry and Barry were hairy.

210

There once lived a certain Miss Gale,
Who turned most exceedingly pale,
  For a mouse climbed her leg
  (Don't repeat this, I beg)
And a splinter got caught in its tail.

211

Said a salty old skipper of Wales,
'Number One, it's all right to chew nails;
  It impresses the crew,
  It impresses me too:
But stop spitting holes in the sails.'

212

How remorselessly time seems to flow
Towards that brave dawn of two oh oh oh.
  As I see the picture,
  The rich will get richer
And, oh yes, some computers will blow.

213

There was a young man of Devizes
Whose ears were of different sizes.
  The one that was small
  Was no use at all,
But the other won several prizes.

214

There was a young fellow of Leeds
Who swallowed a packet of seeds.
  In a month, silly ass,
  He was covered in grass,
And he couldn't sit down for the weeds.

215

A man who came into some money
Decided to marry a bunny.
 But the thought of the ears
 And the tails of the dears
Made him skip it as being too funny.

216

There was an old fellow of Spain,
Whose leg was cut off by a train.
 When his friends said, 'How sad!'
 He replied, 'I am glad,
For I've now lost my varicose veins.'

217

There was a young person named Tate
Took a girl out to eat at 8.08;
 But I will not relate
 What Tate and his date
Ate, *tête-à-tête*, at 8.08.

218

There was an old man of Peru
Who dreamt he was eating his shoe.
 He woke in the night
 In a terrible fright
And found it was perfectly true.

219

There was a young girl of Navarre
In love with a French film star.
 When she followed him over
 From Calais to Dover,
Her friends cried, 'That's going too far!'

220

There was a young girl of Navarre
Who was frightfully fond of a tar.
   When she followed him over
   From Calais to Dover,
Her friends cried, 'That's going too far!'

221

I saw Nelson at the battle of the Nile,
And did the bullets whistle – I should smile!
   And when Pharoah hit the King
   With a cutlass on the wing,
I was lying at the bottom of the pile.

222

There once was a lady of Ryde
Who ate cider apples, and died;
   The apples fermented
   Inside the lamented
To cider inside her inside.

223

There's a very mean man of Belsize
Who thinks he is clever and wise.
   And, what do you think?
   He saves gallons of ink
By simply not dotting his 'i's!

224

We've socially conscious biography,
Aesthetics and social geography;
   Today every field
   Boasts its Marxist yield,
So now we've class-conscious pornography.

225

There once was an artist named Lear
Who wrote verses to make children cheer.
  Though they never made sense
  Their success was immense
And the Queen thought that Lear was a dear.

226

Who tarried in Jericho
Until their beards did grow?
  Judas Iscariot,
  Captain Marryat
And Harriet Martineau.

227

A golfer who came from Calcutta.
Had thoughts much too pungent to utter
  When his wife, as he found
  Ere commencing a round,
Was whisking the eggs with his putter

228

You probably never have heard
Of this rather eccentric old beard
  Who lived in a hole
  In the ground, the poor sole,
To get used to being inteard.

229

There was a stout lady of Cuttack
Posteriorly pecked by a wild duck
  Who pursued her for miles
  And continued his wiles
Till he completely demolished her buttock.

230

'I think,' thought Sam Butler,
'Truth ever lies
  In mean compromise.'
  What could be subtler
Than the thought of Sam Butler?

231

There was a young lady in Natchez
Who fell in some nettlewood patches.
  She sits in her room
  With her bare little moon,
And scratches, and scratches, and scratches.

232

There was a young lady of Dee
Who went down to the river to swim.
  A man in a punt
  Stuck an oar in her eye,
And now she wears glasses, you see.

233

I'm bored to extinction with Harrison,
His limericks and puns are embarrassin'.
  But I'm fond of the bum
  For, though dull as they come,
He makes me feel bright by comparison.

234

A clergyman told from his text
How Samson was scissored and vexed;
  Then a barber arose
  From his sweet Sunday doze
Got rattled, and shouted, 'Who's next?'

235

A creature of charm is the gerbil
Its diet's exclusively herbal;
 It browses all day
 On great bunches of hay,
And farts with an elegant burble.

236

There was a young fellow named Sydney,
Who drank till he ruined his kidney.
 It shrivelled and shrank,
 As he sat there and drank,
But he'd had a good time at it, didn't he?

237

There once was a young girl named Jeanie
Whose dad was a terrible meanie:
 He fashioned a latch
 And a hatch for her snatch –
She could only be had by Houdini.

238

There was a young golfer at Troon
Who always played golf with a spoon.
 'It's handy,' said he,
 'For the brandy, you see,
Should anyone happen to swoon.'

How Clever . . .

❦

1

The great violinist was bowing;
The quarrelsome oarsmen were rowing.
　　But how is the sage
　　To judge from the page:
Was it pigs or seeds that were sowing?

2

A foreigner said, 'I have heard
Your language is really absurd.
　　The spelling is weird,
　　Much worse than I feared,
For word rhymes with bird, nerd or turd.'

3

The Viking had sagas of wore,
Of monsters, and hunting the bar.
　　The poems he sead
　　Were all in his haid;
No wonder his spelling was pour.

4

A Scots sailor, name of McPhie,
Who spoonerised to a degree,
　　Once shouted, 'A wanker!'
　　Instead of, 'Weight anchor!'
And spoke of himself as 'PhcMie'.

5

There was a young farmer from Slough
Who said, 'I've a terrible cough.
  Do you think I should get
  Both the doc and the vet,
Or would one be enough for now?'

6

A waitress on day-shift at Schraffts
Has a couple of interesting craffts.
  She's exceedingly able
  At upsetting the table
And screwing in dumb-waiter schaffts.

7

There was a young man named Colquhoun
Who kept as a pet a babuhoun.
  His mother said, 'Cholmondeley,
  I don't think it's quite colmondeley
To feed your babuhoun with a spuhoun.'

8

Elgar's opera *At the Boar's Head*,
As a title makes no one's face red
  Save Jessica Hood's
  (Most prudish of prudes),
Who thinks of what Spooner'd have said!

9

There was a young poet of Trinity
Who, although he could trill like a linnet, he
  Could never complete
  Any poem with feet,
Saying, 'Idiots,
Can't you see
That what I'm writing
Happens
To be
Free
Verse?'

10

There was a young fellow named Skinner,
Who once took a girl out to dinner.
   At a quarter to nine,
   They sat down to dine.
At a quarter past ten it was in her.
(The dinner, not Skinner.
Skinner was in her before dinner.)

11

The conductor with voice like a hatchet,
Observed to a cellist from Datchet:
   'You have twixt your thighs,
   My dear, a great prize –
An instrument noted for beauty and size –
And yet you just sit there and scratch it!'

12

Said a cat as he playfully threw
His wife down a well in Peru,
   'Relax, dearest Thora,
   Please don't be angora,
I was only artesian you.'

13

A mosquito was heard to complain
That a chemist had poisoned his brain;
   The cause of his sorrow
   Was Paradichloro-
Diphenyltrichlorothane.

14

Whenever he got in a fury, a
Schizophrenic from Upper Manchuria
   Had pseudocyesis,
   Disdiadochokinesis
And haemotoporphyrimuria.

15

It is time to make love, douse the glim;
The evening sky becomes dim
   The stars will soon peep
   As the birds fall asleep;
And the loin shall lie down with the limb.

16

Ethnologists up with the Sioux
Wired home for 'two punts, one canoe'.
   The answer next day
   Said: 'Girls on the way,
But what in hell's name's a "panoe"?'

17

A decrepit old gasman named Peter,
While hunting around his gas heater,
   Touched a leak with his light.
   He rose out of sight –
And, as everyone who knows anything about
    poetry can tell you, he also ruined the meter.

18

We thought him an absolute lamb;
But when he sat down in the jam
   On taking his seat,
   At the Sunday-school treat,
We all heard the vicar say, 'Stand up, please,
    while I say grace.'

19

There was a young lady named Kent,
Who gave up her husband for Lent.
   The night before Easter,
   When Jesus released her,
It didn't make a damned bit of difference because in
    the meantime he'd been running around with a
    whole lot of other women.

20

A bather whose clothing was strewed
By breezes that left her quite nude,
   Saw a man come along
   And, unless I am wrong,
You expected this line to be rude.

21

There was a young man who said, 'Damn!
At last I've found out that I am
   A creature that moves
   In determinate groove:
In fact, not a bus but a tram.'

22

A Christian Scientist, Weighell,
Explained, 'Although pain isn't real,
   If I sit on a pin
   And it punctures my skin,
I dislike what I fancy I feel.'

23

There once was a fellow of Trinity
Who raised xyz to infinity;
   And then the old brute
   Extracted the root.
He afterwards took to Divinity.

24

The fabulous Wizard of Oz
Retired from the business becoz,
   What with up-to-date science,
   To most of his clients
He wasn't the wizard he woz.

25

There was a young lady of Glos
Whose friends quite thought they had los.
  When her handbag they spied
  Coming back from a ride
On the horns of a bull that had tos.

26

A flea and a fly in a flue
Were imprisoned, so what could they do?
  Said the fly: 'Let us flee!'
  Said the flea: 'Let us fly!'
So they flew through a flaw in the flue.

27

A right-handed writer named Wright
In writing 'write' always wrote 'rite',
  When he meant to write 'write'.
  If he'd written 'write' right,
Wright would not have wrought rot writing 'rite'.

28

Said a boy to his teacher one day,
'Wright has not written 'rite' right, I say.'
  And the teacher replied,
  As the error she eyed,
'Right! Wright: write "rite" right, right away!'

29

A loving young couple from Aberystwyth
United the things that they kystwyth.
  But as they grew older
  They also grew bolder,
And united the things that they pystwyth.

30

There was a young lady of Exeter,
So pretty, that men craned their nexeter.
　　One was even so brave
　　As to take out and wave
The distinguishing mark of his sexeter.

31

A sensitive lady from Worcester
At a ball met a fellow who gorcester;
　　A lecherous guy
　　With blood in his uy,
So she ducked out before he sedorcester.

32

There was a young fellow named Fisher
Who was fishing for fish in a fissure;
　　Then a cod with a grin
　　Pulled the fisherman in . . .
Now they're fishing the fissure for Fisher.

33

An effeminate fellow from Lincoln
One night did some serious drincoln,
　　Met a gal, now his wife,
　　Learned the true facts of life,
And blesses the day he got stincoln.

34

A painter who came from Great Britain
Hailed a lady who sat with her knitain.
　　He remarked with a sigh,
　　'That park bench – well, I
Just painted it, right where you're sitain.'

35

Once out on the lake at Dubuque,
A girl took a sail with a duque.
   He remarked, 'I am sure
   You are honest and pure' –
And then leaned far over to puque.

36

A venturesome three-weeks-old chamois
Strayed off in the woods from his mamois.
   And might have been dead
   But some picnickers fed
Him with sandwiches, milk and salamois.

37

A small boy who lived in Iquique
Had a voice irritatingly squique;
   When his father said, 'Oil it,
   My son, or you'll spoil it,'
His retort was a trifle too chique.

38

In a bus queue a jueue bound for Kueue
Thus was hailed by a Scot, whom he knueue:
   'Dinna fash yersel, Lueue,
   I'm paying for yueue!'
And the fueue who o'erheard, whistled, 'Phueue!'

39

An obstinate lady of Leicester
Wouldn't marry her swain, though he preicester.
   For his income, I fear,
   Was a hundred a year,
On which he could never have dreicester.

40

She frowned and called him 'Mr',
Because in sport he kr;
   And so, in spite,
   That very night,
That Mr kr sr.

41

There was a mechalnwick of Alnwick
Whose opinions were anti-Germalnwick.
   So when war had begun
   He went off with a gun
The proportions of which were Titalnwick.

42

A youthful schoolmistress named Beauchamp
Said, 'These awful boys, how shall I teauchamp?
   For they will not behave
   Although I look grave
And with tears in my eyes I beseauchamp.

43

A bald-headed judge named Beauclerk
Fell in love with a maiden seau ferk,
   Residing at Bicester,
   Who said, when he kicester,
'I won't wed a man with neau herk!'

44

There was a young fellow of Beaulieu,
Who loved a fair maiden most treaulieu.
   He said, 'Do be mine,'
   And she didn't decline;
So the wedding was solemnised deaulieu.

45

A charming young lady named Geoghegan,
Whose Christian names are less peophegan,
  Will be Mrs Knollys
  Very soon at All Ksollys;
But the date is at present a veogheg'un.

46

A lady from way down in Ga
Became quite a notable fa.
  But she faded from view
  With a quaint I O U
That she'd signed '(Miss) Lucrezia Ba'.

47

A young man of Gloucester named Foucester,
Had a wife who ran off with a coucester.
  He traced her to Leicester
  And tried to arreicester,
But in spite of these efforts he loucester.

48

An innocent maiden of Gloucester
Fell in love with a coucester named Foucester;
  She met him in Leicester,
  Where he merely careicester,
Then the hard-headed coucester just loucester.

49

A lady, an expert on skis,
Went out with a man who said, 'Plis
  On the next precipice,
  Will you give me a kice?'
She said, 'Quick, before somebody sis!'

50

As he filled up his order book pp.,
He declared, 'I demand higher ww.!'
    So he struck for more pay
    But, alas, they now say
He is sweeping out elephants' cc.

51

There was a young lady named Psyche
Who was heard to ejaculate, 'Pcryche!'
    For when riding her pbych,
    She ran over a ptych,
And fell on some rails that were pspyche.

52

An unskhylful rider from Rhyl
Motor-cycled full speed down a hyl,
    Thyl a sphyl at a bend
    Khyled our whylful young friend,
And he now in the churchyard lies sthyl.

53

A wandering tribe called the Siouxs
Wear moccasins, having no shiouxs
    They are made of buckskin
    With the fleshy side in
Embroidered with beads of bright hiouxs.

54

When out on the warpath, the Siouxs
March single-file, never by tiouxs;
    And by 'blazing' the trees
    Can return at their ease
And their ways through the forests ne'er liouxs.

55

The Honourable Winifred Wemyss
Saw styli and snakes in her dremyss;
 And these she enjeud
 Until she heard Freud
Say: 'Nothing is quite what it semyss.'

56

There was a young lady named Wemyss,
Who it semyss was troubled with dremyss.
 She would wake in the night
 And in terrible fright
Shake the bemyss of her house with her scremyss.

57

There was a young curate of Salisbury
Whose habits were halisbury-scalisbury;
 He'd go hiking in Hampshire
 Without any pampshire
Till the bishop insisted he walisbury.

58

A schoolboy at Sault Ste Marie
Said, 'Spelling is all Greek to me,
 Till they learn to spell "Soo"
 Without any "u"
Or an "a" or an "l" or a "t"!'

59

There was an Arabian sheik
Who entered his harem and speik:
 'A loud cry I heard,
 In here it occurred.
Are my fifty-two children aweik?'

60

A young Englishwoman named St John
Met a red-skinned American It John
   Who made her his bride
   And gave her, beside,
A dress with a gaudy bead Frt John.

61

A certain young chap named Bill Beebee
Was in love with a lady named Phoebe;
   'But,' he said, 'I must see
   What the clerical fee
Be before Phoebe be Phoebe Beebee.'

62

Said a man to his spouse in east Sydenham:
'My best trousers! Now where have you hydenham?
   It is perfectly true
   They were not very new;
But I foolishly left half a quydenham.'

63

There was a young maid in Tahiti
Whom the neighbours considered quite flahiti;
   For if Monday was fine
   She'd hang on the line
An extremely diaphanous nahiti.

64

A young Irish servant in Drogheda
Had a mistress who often annogheda,
   Whereon she would swear
   With language so rare
That thereafter nobody emplogheda.

65

There was a young girl named Cholmondeley,
Witty, warm-hearted and colmondely.
   No girl could be finer,
   But she lacked a vagina –
A sad and arresting anolmondeley.

66

There was a young fellow, named Cholmondeley,
Who always, at dinner, sat dolmondely.
   His fair partner said,
   As he crumbled his bread,
'Dear me! You behave very rolmondeley!'

67

The sermon our bishop, rt revd
Began might have had a rt clevd;
   But his talk though consistent
   Kept the end so far distant,
We left, for we felt he mt nevd.

68

There once was a boring young rev.
Who preached till it seemed he would nev.
   His hearers, *en masse*,
   Got a pain in the ass
And prayed for relief of their neth.

69

A boy who played tunes on a comb
Had become such a nuisance at home
   His ma spanked him, and then,
   'Will you do it again?'
And he cheerfully answered her, 'Nomb.'

70

There was a young lady of Munich
Whose appetite simply was unich.
   She contentedly cooed,
   'There's nothing like food,'
As she let out a tuck ín her tunich.

71

There once was a choleric colonel.
Whose oaths were obscene and infolonel,
   And the chaplain, aghast,
   Gave up protest at last,
But wrote them all down in his jolonel.

72

A fellow who lived in New Guinea,
Was known as a silly young nuinea,
   He utterly lacked
   Good judgement and tacked
For he told a plump girl she was skuinea.

73

Someday ere she grows too antique,
My girl's hand in marriage I'll sicque;
   lf she's not a coquette
   (Which I'd greatly regret),
She shall share my ten dollars a wique.

74

A bright little maid in St Thomas
Discovered a suit of pajhomas.
   Said the maiden, 'Well, well,
   Whose they are I can't tell
But I'm sure that those garments St Mhomas.'

75

There were two young ladies of Birmingham,
And I know a sad story concerningham.
   They stuck needles and pins
   In the right reverend shins
Of the bishop engaged in confirmingham.

76

Said a lively young nursemaid in Padua
To her master, 'Please, sir, you're a dadua.
   I've come for some pins
   For to wrap up the quins
And to hear you remark, sir, how gladua.'

77

There was a young girl in the choir,
Whose voice rose hoir and hoir,
   Till it reached such a height
   It was clear out of seight,
And they found it next day in the spoir.

78

A barber who lived in Batavia.
Was known for his fearless behavia.
   An enormous baboon
   Broke in his saloon,
But he murmured, 'I'm damned if I'll shavia.'

79

There was a composer named Liszt
Whose music no one could resiszt.
   When he swept the keyboard
   Nobody could be bored,
And now that he's gone he is miszt.

80

There once was a gnu in a zoo
Who tired of the same daily view.
　　To seek a new sight,
　　He stole out one night,
And where he went, gnobody gnew.

81

We've got a new maid called Chrysanthemum
Who said, 'I have just come from Grantham, m'm.
　　I lost my last place
　　In the sorest disgrace,
'Cos I snored through the National Anthem, m'm.'

82

An eccentric old lady of Honiton
(Whose conduct I once wrote a sonnet on)
　　Has now been in bed
　　With a cold in her head,
For a week, with her boots and her bonnet on.

83

There was a fair maiden of Warwick
Who lived in the castle histarwick.
On the damp castle mould
She contracted a could,
And the doctor prescribed paregarwick.

84

There was a young woman of Welwyn
Loved a barman, who served in the Belwyn.
　　But the Belwyn, oh dear!
　　Had a welwyn the rear,
So they never were wed, for they felwyn.

85

There once was an African Mau-Mau
Got into a rather bad row-row.
   The cause of the friction?
   His practising diction,
Saying: 'How-how now-now brown-brown cow-cow?'

86

There was a young lassie of Lancashire
Who landed a job as a bank cashier:
   But as she hardly knew
   $1 + 1 = 2$,
She had to give place to a man cashier.

87

The Devil, who plays a deep part,
Has tricked his way into your heart
   By simple insistence
   On his non-existence –
Which really is devilish smart.

88

There was a young lady of Stornoway
Who, through walking, her feet had quite worn away.
   Said she, 'I don't mind,
   For I think I might find
A most troublesome corn will have gone away.'

89

There was a young man of Japan,
Who wrote verses that never would scan.
   When folk told him so,
   He replied: 'Yes, I know,
But I always try and get as many words into the
    last line as I possibly can.'

90

Riverrun where can you guess?
Finnegan's Wake is a mess.
    Will you help me get even?
    Said left-over Stephen.
Yes I said yes I will Yes.

91

As Bradley is said to have said,
'If I think that I'm lying in bed
    With this girl that I feel
    And can touch, is it real?
Or just going on in my head?'

92

There was a young lady from Powys,
Who asked of her lover, 'Just howys
    It possible for you
    To perform as you do?
Quoth he, 'An amalgam of ability and prowys.'

93

When you think of the hosts without no.
Who are slain by the deadly cuco.
    It's such a mistake
    Of such food to partake:
It results in a permanent slo.

94

An unpopular man of Cologne
With a pain in his stomach did mogne;
He heaved a great sigh,
And said: 'I would digh,
But the loss would be simply my ogne.'

95

'I wouldn't be bothered with drawers,'
Says one of our better-known whawers.
    'There isn't a doubt
    I'm better without,
In handling my everyday chawers.'

96

There was a young lady named Bright
Who travelled far faster than light,
    She set out one day
    In a relative way,
And returned on the previous night.

97

There was a young man of Nepal
Who had a mathematical ball;
    $(W^3 \times \pi) - 8 = \frac{4}{3} \sqrt{0}$ – The cube of its weight,
    Times pi, minus eight,
Is four thirds of the root of fuck all.

98

'The order of nature,' quoth he,
'Is wondrously brought home to me
    When I think that my clock
    With each tick and each tock
Goes $2\pi\sqrt{\frac{1}{g}}$ [two pi times the root of L over G].

99

An assistant professor named Ddodd
Had manners arresting and odd.
    He said, 'If you please,
    Spell my name with four d's.'
Though one was sufficient for God.

Artists

❦

1

Said the Duchess of Alba to Goya:
'Paint some pictures to hang in my foya!'
   So he painted her twice:
   In the nude, to look nice,
And then in her clothes, to annoya.

2

Whilst Titian was mixing rose madder,
His model posed nude on a ladder.
   Her position to Titian
   Suggested coition
So he climbed up the ladder and had her.

3

A curious artist, Picasso:
His voice was remarkably basso,
   His balls were both cubic,
   His hair was all pubic.
Some thought him a bit of an arsehole.

4

While viewing a painting of Venus,
A young student added a penis.
   He had to erase it:
   He'd been asked to praise it.
At least he's found out what a paean is!

5

In his youth our old friend Boccaccio
Was having a girl in a patio.
    When it came to the twat
    She wasn't so hot,
But, boy, was she good at fellatio!

6

Of a sudden, the great prima donna
Cried: 'Gawd: my voice is a gonner.'
    But a cat in the wings
    Said: 'I know how she sings,'
And finished the solo with honour.

7

There was a young lady named Hatch
Who doted on music by Bach.
    She played with her pussy
    To *The Faun* by Debussy,
But to ragtime she just scratched her snatch.

8

There's a sensitive type in Tom's River
Whom Beethoven causes to quiver;
    The aesthetic vibration
    Brings soulful elation.
And also is fine for the liver.

9

A *musicienne* in gay Montebello
Amused herself playing the cello,
    But not a solo,
    For she used as a bow
The dong of a sturdy young fellow.

10

A baritone star of Havana
Slipped horribly on a banana;
   He was sick for a year
   Then resumed his career –
As a promising lyric soprano.

11

It was hard on Apollo, I thought,
When the workman who shifted him caught
   And broke off his penis,
   From malice or meanness,
And shipped him to England with naught.

12

There once was a sculptor named Phidias
Who had a distate for the hideous;
   So he sculpt Aphrodite
   Without any nightie,
Which shocked the ultra-fastidious.

13

A sculptor of Pop-Art named Jock
Intends each new statue to shock.
   Outsize genitalia
   Gave the critics heart-failure,
But the public said, 'Pure poppy-cock!'

14

A sculptor remarked: 'I'm afraid
I have fallen in love with my trade.
   I'm much too elated
   With what I've created,
But chiefly the women I've made.'

15

The Grecians were famed for fine art
And buildings and stonework so smart.
  They distinguished with poise
  The men from the boys
And used crowbars to keep them apart.

16

For sculpture that's really first class
You need form, composition and mass.
  To carve a good Venus
  Just leave off the penis
And concentrate all on the ass.

17

We was took by our teacher, Miss Beeham,
To see statues in't British Museum.
  Us girls was in fits
  'Cos the int'resting bits
Of the boys was broke off – you should see 'em!

18

There's a wonderful family called Stein:
There's Gert and there's Ep and there's Ein.
  Gert's poems are bunk,
  Ep's statues are junk,
And no one can understand Ein.

19

There was a young man of Cape Race,
Whose mind was an utter disgrace;
  He thought Marie Corelli
  Lived long before Shelley,
And that Wells was the name of a place.

20

Ivy Compton-Burnett's irritations,
And the titles she gives her narrations.
   All these misses and misters,
   All those *Brothers and Sisters* –
They all sound like sexual relations.

21

There once was a couple named Mound
Whose sexual control was profound:
   When engaged in coition,
   They had the ambition
To study the *Cantos* by Pound.

22

There was a young poet of Thusis,
Who went twilight walks with the Muses,
   But the nymphs of the air
   Are not what they were
And the practice has led to abuses.

23

Word has come down from the dean
That by use of the teaching machine
   Old Oedipus Rex
   Could have learned about sex
Without ever disturbing the queen.

24

'I would doubt,' said the Bishop of Balham,
'Whether Tennyson ever screwed Hallam.
   Such things are best hid.
   Let us hope that he did:
De mortuis nil nisi malum.'

25

There was a young fellow of Buckingham,
Wrote a treatise on cunts and on sucking them.
   But later this work
   Was eclipsed by a Turk
Whose topic was assholes and fucking them.

26

If you find for your verse there's no call,
And you can't afford paper at all,
   For the poet true born,
   However forlorn,
There's always the lavatory wall.

27

A limerick writer named Symes
Said, 'I'm so frustrated at times:
   I can do –ock and –uck,
   But with –unt I get stuck.
I'm really quite hopeless with rhymes.'

28

There was an anthologist who
Decided that nought was taboo.
   Her words are so rude,
   Her verses so lewd,
I'm sure they'll appeal to you.

29

Well it's partly the shape of the thing
That gives the old limerick wing.
   Those accordion pleats
   Full of airy conceits
Take it up like a kite on a string.

30

At Harvard, a randy old dean
Said: 'The funniest jokes are obscene.
  To bowdlerise wit
  Takes the shit out of it –
Who wants a limerick clean?'

31

The lady in search of five-liners
Quite covered the table for diners
  With horrible scraps
  Of sexual mishaps
Of those who agreed and decliners.

32

There was a sweet lady with specs
Who fought to find lines without sex.
  She covered the table
  With all she was able
To pinch without copyright cheques.

33

The limerick's callous and crude,
Its morals distressingly lewd;
  It's not worth the reading
  By persons of breeding –
It's designed for us vulgar and rude.

34

An eccentric young poet named Brown
Raised up his embroiderèd gown
  To look for his peter
  To beat it to metre,
But fainted when none could be found.

35

An authoress, armed with a skewer,
Once hunted a hostile reviewer.
　　'I'll teach him,' she cried,
　　'When I've punctured his hide,
To call my last novel too pure.'

36

The cross-eyed old painter McNeff
Was colour-blind, palsied and deaf.
　　When he asked to be touted,
　　The critics all shouted:
'This is art, with a capital F!'

37

'My girlfriend wants me to ski,'
Said the flabby young cellist, 'but Gee!
　　With Stravinsky, Stokowski,
　　Mussorgsky, Tchaikovsky,
That's quite enough skiing for me.'

Some Political Musings

❦

1

SINGLE-PARENT FAMILIES

Though we've beaten the Soviet scum
And castrated his trade-union chum,
    What may yet overwhelm
    The defence of the realm
Is the threat of the unmarried mum.

2

LIB-DEMS

Oh the Lib-Dems are searching the land for
The breakthrough they've long hoped and
    planned for,
    But what gets in their way
    Is that not even they
Have the slightest idea what they stand for.

3

THE TORY LEADERSHIP

'Tell me, Peter,' said Michael Portillo,
As he polished his smile with a Brillo,
    'Will I ever ascend
    To the greasy pole's end?
No, don't answer: keep chewing that pillow.'

4

NHS

I'm jolly, I'm nice, I'm Virginia,
And my thinking is pleasingly linear.
    If you look a bit green, I'll
    Just class you as senile,
Then so long, *au revoir*, I'll be seein' ya.

5

NORTHERN IRELAND

My poll ratings were plummeting crazily,
I just came across greyly and hazily,
    It was time to strongarm
    One with even less charm
And God sent me the Reverend Paisley.

6

HERITAGE

Have the treasures of landscape and hall
Any chance of survival at all,
    With Jocelyn Stevens
    No better than evens
And with Rifkind two fifths of . . . quite small?

7

LAW AND ORDER

Yes, crime: that's the wicket we'll bat on;
These yobboes must firmly be sat on.
    We'll raise a new breed
    Without aggro or greed
With role models like Lilley, Clarke, Patton.

8

ROADS

Some time back, we were worried as hell
That the railways might start to do well.
   Now that could cost loads
    To our friends who build roads,
So we sent for Bob Horton from Shell.

9

TORY MORALITY

The thing about 'Back to basics'
And similar high moral tricks
   Is they're bound to backfire
    When your angelic choir
Have all got their brains in their dicks.

10

WHERE THE WORD 'TORY' CAME FROM

There's an old Irish word meaning 'thief' –
Four letters, quite pithy and brief.
   I tell you no lie,
    It is T–O–R–Y,
Now doesn't that bugger belief?

Irish Limericks

❦

1

Is duine me' dhio'las leann la'
'S chuireas mo bhuio'n chum remcais;
Mura mbeadh duine iim chuideachta dhio'lfas
Mise bheas thio's leis in anthra'th.

O'Tuama (John O'Tuomy, 1706–77)

I sell the best brandy and sherry
To make my good customers merry;
    But at time their finances
    Run short as it chances
And then I feel very sad, very.

TRANSLATION

2

Here's brandy! Come fill up your tumbler,
Or ale if your liking be humbler,
    And while you've a shilling
    Keep filling and swilling,
A fig for the growls of the grumbler.

John O'Tuomy

3

I like when I'm quite at my leisure
Mirth music and all sorts of pleasure.
  When Margery's bringing
  The glass, I like singing
With bards, if they drink within measure.

JOHN O'TUOMY

4

The time I've lost in wooing,
In watching and pursuing
  The light that lies
  In women's eyes
Has been my heart's undoing.
Though wisdom oft has sought me,
I scorned the lore she brought me,
  My only books
  Were women's looks
And folly's all they've taught me.

THOMAS MOORE (1779–1852)

5

Oh the sight entrancing
When morning's beam is glancing
  O'er files arrayed
  With helm and blade
And plumes in the gay wind dancing.
When hearts are all high beating
And the trumpet's voice repeating
  That song whose breath
  May lead to death
But never to retreating.

THOMAS MOORE

6

Leave pomps to those who need 'em,
Adorn but man with Freedom
   And proud he braves
   The gaudiest slaves
That crawl where monarch lead 'em.

THOMAS MOORE

7

O' Tuomy you boast yourself handy
At selling good ale and bright brandy;
   But the fact is your liquor
   Makes everyone sicker –
I tell you that, I, your friend Andy.

But your poems and pints, by your favour,
Are alike wholly wanting in flavour.
   Because it's your pleasure,
   You give us short measure –
And your ale has a ditchwater savour.

You bow to the floor's very level
When customers enter to revel,
   But if one in shy raiment
   Takes a drink without payment
You'll score it against the poor devil!

8

A young lassie from sweet Ballybunion
Whose kisses were sweeter than honey,
   The Irishmen galore
   Would line up at her door
All willing to pay her some money.

9

There was a young fellow named Barney
Who wanted to visit Killarney
   He was told the colleens there
   Were screwing machines there
But found it was Irishman's blarney.

10

A priest who got up with the dawn,
Saw a lass near a bush in Gougane,
   'Excuse me, dear miss,
   It's sinful to piss
On the sacred and blessed green lawn.'

11

A lassie at Cahermee Fair,
Was having her first love affair.
   As she climbed into bed
   To the tinker she said:
'Do you mind if I start with a prayer?'

12

To an Irishman landing in Heaven
Said St Peter: 'We dine sharp at seven.
   Then breakfast's at eight,
   Never mind if you're late,
And there's Irish crubeens at eleven.'

13

There was a young lass from Rosscarbery,
Who started to count every calorie.
   Said her boss in disgust:
   'If you lose half your bust –
Then you're worth only half of your salary.'

14

There was a young lady near Glin
Who was strong on Original Sin.
 The priest said: 'Do be good,'
 She said: 'I would if I could.'
And started all over again.

15

A lass on the road to Goleen
Met a baker with a drop of poteen,
 Five minutes of lovin'
 Put a bun in her oven,
The next time she won't be so keen.

16

A young lass on a yacht in Glandore,
So tired she could do it no more.
 'But I'm willing to try
 So where shall I lie?
On the deck, on the sail, or the floor?'

17

There was a young lass from Listowel,
Whose beauty was everyone's goal,
 In her efforts to please
 Spread a well-known disease
From Slea Head to the frosty South Pole.

18

There was a young man near Dunowen,
Who strolled by himself all alone.
 He's a face like a hatchet,
 I defy you to match it,
Said he: 'I don't mind, it's my own.'

19

There was an old monk from Kilcrea,
Who of fasting grew tired every day.
  Till at length with a yell,
  He burst from his cell.
'From now on I'm going to be gay.'

20

There was a young lass from near Middleton
Who had such a very short skirt on
  That the curate said: 'Dear,
  You look very queer.
Have you really a skirt or a shirt on?'

21

There was a young blade from near Youghal,
Who found he had only one ball.
  Obsessed by his wants,
  He discarded his pants.
In his kilts he is now loved by all.

22

A farmer from Newcastlewest,
Who courted a maiden with zest,
  So hard did he press her,
  To make her say, 'Yes, sir,'
That he broke the ould watch in his vest.

23

In Ireland a young guard on the beat,
Saw a couple more fond than discreet.
  'Though a Miss, miss a kiss,
  Give the next kiss a miss –
For a kiss is amiss in the street.'

24

A woman from near Templenoe,
Her husband was awfully slow,
   They kept at it all night,
   And got everything right,
For practice makes pregnant, you know!

25

A lassie from Borriskane
Who went and undressed in a train,
   A saucy old porter,
   Saw more than he ought-er,
And asked her to do it again!

26

'Far dearer to me than my treasure,'
An Irish lassie said, 'is my leisure,
   For then I can screw,
   Each rich yachtman's crew –
They're slow but it lengthens the pleasure.'

27

There once was a lassie from Bandon,
Who said to her man: 'Keep your hand on,
   I admire your technique,
   It's simply unique,
But my breasts are to love – not to land on.'

28

There once was a boring Irish priest,
Whose sermons one felt never ceased.
   His hearers, *en masse*,
   Got fatigued to the ass,
And slept through the most sacred Feast.

29

A lassie from this side of Rathmore,
Was wed to one hell of a bore –
    A dopey old farmer,
    Too lazy to warm her,
All he did every night was just snore.

30

A young Irish farmer named Willy,
Whose behaviour was frequently silly,
    At a big farmers' ball,
    Dressed in nothing at all –
He claimed he came there as a filly.

31

There was a young lassie from Crosser,
Who in spiritual things was a messer.
    When sent to the priest,
    This lewd little beast,
Did her best to seduce her confessor.

32

Two tourists at fair Salthill Strand
Who tried to make love on the sand,
    The Garda on duty
    Said: 'No, me proud beauties,
Them foreign contortions is banned.'

33

A young Irish lad like a giant
Who in sexual ways was just quaint,
    One day he went swimming
    With twelve naked women
And deserted them all for a pint.

34

In the village that's well known as Leap
The girls there would sure give one pep.
  They've a wonderful carriage
  And are red-ripe for marriage,
Don't go further if you're taking that step.

35

In the crags near the wild Mizen Head
Sure the couples you'd swear they were wed.
  They lose all their shame
  And forget their good name
For they think that the grass is the bed.

36

Near the sea by the famed Inchydoney
Some sights you will see there are funny,
  The lovers together,
  Bobbing up in the heather,
And the clergy play cards for the money.

37

Oh I'd love to live near Adrigole
And draw fifty a week on the dole,
  And to hear the birds sing
  And the waterfalls ring
And a big cosy fire of free coal.

38

To the gay town of old Skibbereen,
Came a tinker abnormally lean;
  They fed him so well,
  That he started to swell,
And by Christmas he looked like a dean.

39

I'm saying me prayers to St Jude
To keep away thoughts that are lewd.
   He'll do what he can
   To get me a man
And we'll wed, and we'll bed, is that rude?

40

Oh I love to stop off in Millstreet
And sample the poteen so neat,
   For despite the poor guards
   It's made in backyards
While they walk in the cold on the beat.

41

In the Gaeltacht of sweet Ballingearry,
Where the Gaels of both sexes are airy,
   If you want to make love
   It's OK from Above
If you do it through Irish – and be wary!

42

A baritone who strolled near Falcarragh
Slipped one day on a yellow banana.
   He was shagged for a year
   But once more did appear,
This time as a rousing soprano!

43

A lass on the island of Clear
Once knelt in the moonlight all bare,
   She prayed to her God,
   For a bit on the sod,
And a hippy boy answered her prayer!

44

A young man near the Bridge of Blackwater,
Who daily got shorter and shorter,
  'The reason,' he said,
  'Is the brains in me head
Get so heavy that I fear a disorder.'

45

There's a wood near the fair Castlefreke
Where short-taken gents sometimes leak
  If you've been well brought up
  And are not a pup
Of the strange things you'll see, you'll ne'er speak.

46

A lassie from near Dromahilly,
Had a craving to walk Piccadilly,
  She said: 'Ain't it funny?
  It ain't for the money!
But if I don't take it it's silly.'

47

There's a sweet little place Courtmacsherry,
You can get there by road or by ferry.
  Some girls wear no panties
  Or other such scanties
But most have held on to their cherry.

48

There was an old lady from Mallow,
Whose complexion was just very sallow,
  When asked for the cause,
  She replied without pause –
'Sure, three times a day I chew tallow!'

49

A tourist at fair Galway Bay,
Made fireworks on a hot summer's day.
  He dipped his cigar
  In the gunpowder jar,
Now the fish have got fat in the bay!

50

There was a young lad from Clengarriff,
Who liked to dress up as a sheriff.
  He toted his guns,
  Swore he'd save all the nuns
From the guys who looked like Omar Sharif!

51

Sure, I'm living in Ballydehob,
Away from that damn city mob.
  I go to Confession,
  Attend every Mission,
Say the Rosary each night by the hob!

52

An Irishman with a long beard,
Who said: 'It is just as I feared –
  Two Cocks and a Hen
  Four Ducks and a Wren
Have all built their nests in my beard!'

53

I'm in love with a lass near Ardfert,
Whose hair is so scant it won't part.
  She's cross-eyed and thin,
  And as ugly as sin.
But then, she has such a good heart!

54

There was a young lady from Cork,
Whose Da made a fortune in pork!
 He got for his daughter
 A Derry husband who taught her
To balance green peas on her fork!

55

A tourist in Kerry named Jones,
Who reduced many Roses to moans
 By his wonderful knowledge,
 Found out while in college
Of women's most ticklesome zones.

56

There was a young man from West Cork
Whose Da made a fortune in pork.
 Last Sunday at three,
 He was married to me –
Because we're expecting the stork!

57

A man from the wild Blasket Isles,
Who suffered severely from piles,
 He couldn't sit down
 For fear he would drown
So he had to row standing for miles.

58

A big ship came into Cork Quay,
Full of sailors just mad for a lay!
 The whores of the city
 Rushed on board without pity,
In their hurry they smashed the gangway.

59

A young lass from near to Ardkeragh
Whose body had plenty of meat there.
   She said: 'Marry me fast,
   And you'll find that my ass
Is the spot for to warm your cold feet there.'

60

The thoughts of the rabbits on sex
Are seldom if ever complex.
   For up on Cape Clear
   They make love without fear,
And do just as a Gaelgoir expects.

61

How sad for to see Baltimore!
Where the Irish are now to the fore.
   God be with the old days
   And our dear British ways –
But, alas and alack, they're no more!

62

In Ballybunion some visitors will go
To see what no person should know.
   But then there are tourists
   The purest of purists –
Who say 'tis uncommonly low!

63

In Donnybrook dwells a strange race
So far from the Queen – what disgrace!
   But they strive to be merry,
   With pre-dinner sherry –
And they toast her, and roast her, with grace!

64

A woman who lived outside Cobh,
Got a notion to marry, by Jove.
    She nabbed a young sailor.
    Who swore he'd ne'er fail her,
Which ended his days on the rove!

65

There's a lassie from Castletownbere,
With tresses of lovely dark hair,
    Which I'd love to be feeling,
    And sweet kisses stealing,
And that little bit more – sure I'd dare!

66

Said a missioner in Old Ballycotton,
'The waltz of the devil's begotten!'
    Said Jones to Miss Joy,
    'Never mind the ould guy,
To the pure almost everything's rotten!'

67

A farmer from Ballymacoda,
Was awarded a special diploma
    For telling apart
    A masculine fart
From a similar female aroma!

68

A lass from the town of Portnoo
Found love-making affected her hue.
    She presented to sight
    Her face pink, her breasts white –
And another part – red, black and blue.

69

And here's to the good old Cape Clear –
Where long after midnight flows beer.
   And the Capers so gay
    Work twelve hours a day –
At free grants and free dole they just jeer!

70

A man from Achill Island said: 'Do
Tell me how I can add two and two?
   I'm not very sure
    That it doesn't make four –
But I fear that is always too few.'

71

There is a creator named God,
Whose doings are sometimes quite odd.
   He made Kerrymen cute,
    And Tipperarymen mute,
Which when all's said and done is just cod!

72

A tourist just near Dunamark,
Who, when he made love, had to bark.
   His wife was a bitch,
    With a terrible itch –
So, Glengarriff can't sleep after dark!

73

A pretty young lass from Kilquane
While walking was caught in the rain.
   She ran – almost flew.
    Her complexion did too!
And she reached home exceedingly plain.

74

A young lass on the fair stand of Howe,
Who said that she didn't know how.
   Then an Irishman caught her,
   And bloody soon taught her,
And did it without any row.

75

A lass from the City of Cork,
Was shortly expecting the 'stork'.
   When the doctor walked in
   With a businesslike grin,
A pickaxe, a spade, and a fork.

76

'Twas an Irish farmer who said,
'Can I take off me leggin's in bed?'
   His brother said: 'No.
   Wherever you go,
You must wear them until you are dead.'

77

A farmer from near Ballineen,
Who grew so abnormally lean.
   And flat and compressed,
   That his back squeezed his chest,
And sideways he couldn't be seen.

78

A lassie from near to Stradbally
Who is worried by lovers so many
   That the saucy young elf
   Means to raffle herself,
And the tickets are two for a penny!

79

A young man from near Carrighart
Known from Cork to Fair Head for his farts.
    When they asked: 'Why so loud?'
    He replied with head bowed:
'When I farts, sure I farts from the heart.'

80

Said a girl making love in a shanty:
'My dear, your legs are all slanty.'
    He replied: 'I can use
    Any angle I choose.
I do as I please – I'm from Bantry!'

81

A lass from the town of Macroom
Made love to the Man in the Moon.
    'Well, it has been great fun,'
    She remarked when 'twas done,
'But I'm sorry to leave him so soon.'

82

A young lass from near Lisbellaw
Was hurt by her low strapless bra,
    She loosened one wire
    Whereupon the entire
Dress fell – Guess what the RUC saw?

83

Every time an Irish 'county type' swoons,
Her breasts they pop out like balloons.
    But her butler stands by
    With hauteur in his eye,
And puts them back gently with spoons!

84

An Irish lass loves not her lover
So much as she loves his love of her.
   Then loves she her lover
   For love of her lover,
Or love of her love of her lover?

85

There was a blackguard from near Croom,
Who lured a poor girl to her doom.
   He not only seduced her,
   But robbed her and goosed her.
And left her to pay for the room.

86

There once was a lass from Banteer,
So enormously large that, oh dear –
   Once far out in the ocean
   She made such a commotion,
That the Russians torpedoed her rear.

87

A farmer from near Skibbereen,
Who was terribly haughty and mean;
   When women were nigh,
   He'd unbutton his fly,
And shout, 'Look – 'tis fit for the Queen.'

88

At a fancy-dress dance in Tahilla,
A tourist went there as a pillow.
   When the feathers fell out,
   It revealed to the crowd,
That as clothing the dress was a killer.

89

A lass near the bay of Blacksod
Thought babies were made up by God!
   But 'twas not the Almighty
   Who pulled up her nightie,
'Twas a clot from Valentia, by God

90

A lassie from Liscannor Bay,
Was asked to make love in the hay.
   She jumped at the chance,
   But held on to her pants.
For she never had tried it that way!

91

Sure, I dine at the best spot in Cork,
On the best of pig's head and of pork,
   I eat spuds and boiled eggs,
   And turkey-cocks legs,
And I don't have to use knife or fork!

92

Near the barracks there lives a young lass,
Who is said to have two breasts of brass.
   A soldier who bit her,
   Found in one a transmitter!
For she works for the news house of Tass!

93

In Belfast dwelt a sweet maid,
Who swore that she wasn't afraid,
   But a farmer from Derry
   Came after her cherry –
'Twasn't just an advance – 'twas a raid!

94

In the ancient old town of Kinsale,
Where there's lashin's of beer and of ale,
   Where each man despite strife,
   Lives with his own wife.
If you've heard something else – it's a tale!

95

In Waterford town on the dole,
At last I have reached my life's goal.
   With a hundred a week
   No TD has the cheek
To ask me to work, bless their soul!

96

A farmer from near to Croagh Patrick
Who strangled his wife with a halter,
   Said he: 'I won't bury her,
   She'll do for the terrier,
So I'll hide her, and clean her, and salt her.'

97

There was a young tourist in Eskine,
Whose looks admiration did win.
   When I said to her: 'Grace,
   You'd look nice in lace,'
Said, 'In fact, I look best in my skin.'

98

A lass a few miles from Ardfert,
Used to jog till her corns they did hurt,
   But now she just stands
   In the square on her hands
With her head covered up by her skirt.

99

A young lad from outside Dunleary
Of girls was exceedingly wary,
  Till a tourist, named Lou,
  Showed him how and with who
He could make the long evenings more cheery!

100

A woman from sweet Donegal
Had triplets almost each fall.
  She was asked how and wherefore?
  Said: 'Sure, that's what we're here for,
But betimes we got nothing at all.'

101

A lassie from near Carbery's Isle,
Had the ugliest bottom for miles.
  But a blacksmith took pity
  And made it quite pretty,
All dimples and poutings and smiles!

Limerick Sequences

❧

THEY A' DO'T

The grit folk an' the puir do't,
The blyte folk an' the sour do't,
   The black, the white,
   Rude an' polite,
Baith autocrat an' boor do't.

For they a' do't – they a' do't,
The beggars an' the braw do't,
   Folk that ance were,
   An' folk that are –
The folk that come will a' do't.

   The auld folk try't
   The young ane's spy't,
An' straightway kiss an' fa' to't,
   The blind, the lame,
   The wild, the tame,
In warm climes an' in cauld do't.

The licensed by the law to't,
Forbidden folk an' a' do't,
   An' priest an' nun
   Enjoy the fun,
An' never ance say na' to't.

The goulocks an' the snails do't,
The cushie-doos an' quails do't,
   The dogs, the cats,
   The mice, the rats,
E'en elephants an' whales do't.

The weebit cocks an' hens do't,
The robins an' the wrens do't,
   The grizzy bears,
   The toads an' hares,
The puddocks in the fens do't.

The boars an' kangaroos do't,
The titlins an' cuckoos do't,
   While sparrows sma'
   An' rabbits a'
In countless swarms an' crews do't.

The midges, fleas, an' bees do't,
The mawkes an' mites in cheese do't,
   An' cault earthworms
   Crawl up in swarms,
An' underneath the trees do't.

The kings an' queens an' a' do't,
The sultan an' pacha do't,
   An' Spanish dons
   Loup off their thrones,
Pu' doon their breeks, an' fa' to't.

For they a' do't – they a' do't,
The grit as weel's the sma' do't,
   Frae crowned king
   To creeping thing,
'Tis just the same – they a' do't!

2

ROYAL SPASM IN FIVE FITS

Thus spake the King of Siam:
'For women I don't care a damn.
  But a fat-bottomed boy
  Is my pride and my joy –
They call me a bugger: I am.'

'Indeed,' quoth the King of Siam,
'For cunts I just don't give a damn.
  They haven't the grip,
  Nor the velvety tip,
Nor the scope of the asshole of man.'

Then up spake the Bey of Algiers
And said to his harem, 'My dears,
  You may think it odd 'f me
  But I've given up sodomy –
Tonight there'll be fucking!' (*Loud cheers*)

Then up spake the young King of Spain:
'To fuck and to bugger is pain.
  But it's not *infra dig*
  On occasion to frig,
And I do it again and again.'

Then up spoke a Hindu mahout,
And said, 'What's all this blithering about?
  Why, I shoot my spunk
  Up an elephant's trunk – '
(*Cries of* 'Shame! He's a shit! Throw him out!')

3

There was an old man of Nantucket
Who kept all his cash in a bucket.
  His daughter, called Nan,
  Ran away with a man,
And as for the bucket, Nantucket.

Pa followed the pair to Pawtucket
(The man and the girl with the bucket),
  And he said to the man
  'You're welcome to Nan!'
But as for the bucket, Pawtucket.

Then the pair followed Pa to Manhasset,
Where he still held the cash as an asset;
  And Nan and the man
  Stole the money and ran,
And as for the bucket, Manhasset.

4

OVER THERE

Oh, the peters they grow small, over there,
Oh, the peters they grow small, over there,
  Oh, the peters they grow small,
  Because they work 'em for a fall,
And then eats 'em, tops and all, over there.

Oh, the pussies they are small, over there,
Oh, the pussies they are small, over there,
  Oh, the pussies they are small,
  But they take 'em short and tall,
And then burns their pricks and all, over there.

Oh, I wish I was a pimp, over there,
Oh, I wish I was a pimp, over there,
   Oh, I wish I was a pimp,
   For I'd give the boys a crimp,
With all my whorey blimps, over there.

Oh, they had a squirt for clap, over there,
Oh, they had a squirt for clap, over there,
   Oh, they had a squirt for clap,
   It was a potent clap trap,
And it burnt our pecker's cap, over there.

5

IN MOBILE

Oh, the men they wash the dishes, in Mobile,
Oh, the men they wash the dishes, in Mobile,
   Oh, the men they wash the dishes,
   And they dry them on their britches,
Oh, the dirty sons-of-bitches, in Mobile!

Oh, the cows they all are dead, in Mobile,
Oh, the cows they all are dead, in Mobile,
   Oh, the cows they all are dead,
   So they milk the bulls instead,
Because babies must be fed, in Mobile!

Oh, they teach the babies tricks, in Mobile,
Oh, they teach the babies tricks, in Mobile,
   Oh, they teach the babies tricks,
   And by the time that they are six,
They suck their fathers' pricks in Mobile!

Oh, the eagles they fly high, in Mobile,
Oh, the eagles they fly high, in Mobile,
   Oh, the eagles they fly high
   And from way up in the sky,
They shit squarely in your eye, in Mobile!

6

MOTOR VERSE

You'll never never know how good you are
Till you try to make love in a car.
   Many a man meets defeat
   On a darkened back seat,
It's only the experts break par.

A fellow from old Copenhagen
Wooed a girl in his little Volkswagen;
   But the damage was high:
   The stick-shift in his eye,
And a gash from the dash in his noggin'.

A guy with a girl in a Fiat
Asked, 'Where on earth is my key at?'
   When he started to seek
   She let out a shriek:
'That's not where it's likely to be at!'

They sat in his little old Lloyd,
Frustrated, and hot, and annoyed;
   But enough of palaver:
   He attempted to have 'er
And the car was entirely destroyed.

There once was a fellow named Brett
Loved a girl in his shiny Corvette;
   We know it's absurd
   But the last that we heard
They hadn't untangled them yet.

Said a man of his small Morris Minor:
'For petting, it couldn't be finer;
   But for love's consummation
   A wagon called station
Would offer a playground diviner.'

7

THAT OLD APPLE TREE

In the shade of the old apple tree
Where between her fat legs I could see
   A little brown spot
   With the hair in a knot,
And it certainly looked good to me.

I asked as I tickled her tit
If she thought that my big thing would fit.
   She said it would do
   So we had a good screw
In the shade of the old apple tree.

In the shade of the old apple tree
I got all that was coming to me.
   In the soft dewy grass
   I had a fine piece of ass
From a maiden that was fine to see.

I could hear the dull buzz of the bee
As he sunk his grub hooks into me.
   Her ass it was fine
   But you should have seen mine
In the shade of the old apple tree.

from The Cremorne Magazine, *1882*

❦

1

A festive young lady of Wick,
While sucking her grandfather's prick,
   Exclaimed, 'I don't funk
   The taste of your spunk,
It's the smell of your arse makes me sick.'

2

There was a young lady of Brighton
Whose c–u–n–t was a tight'n.
   If you give a good shove,
   It will fit like a glove,
But, excuse me, you're not in the right 'n.

3

There was a young lady of Reading,
Who got poxed, and the virus kept spreading.
   Her nymphae each day
   Kept on sloughing away
Till at last you could shove your whole head in.

4

There was a young man of Soho,
Whose tastes were exceedingly low.
　He said to his mother,
　Let us suck one another,
And swallow the seminal flow.

5

There was a young man of Rheims,
Who was subject to wet dreams.
　He bottled a dozen
　And sent to his cousin,
And labelled them 'chocolate creams'.

Of Maiden Aunts and Virgin Girls

❧

1

There once was a spinster of Ealing,
Endowed with such delicate feeling,
   That she thought that a chair
   Should not have its legs bare,
So she kept her eyes fixed on the ceiling.

2

A near-sighted spinster named White
Wore a suit of pyjamas one night;
   As she happened to pass
   In front of the glass,
She exclaimed, 'There's a man!' in delight.

3

There was an old maid of Pitlochry
Whose morals were truly a mockery,
   For under the bed
   Was a lover instead
Of the usual porcelain crockery.

4

A certain old maid in Cohoes
In despair taught her bird to propose;
   But the parrot, dejected
   At being accepted,
Spoke some lines too profane to disclose.

5

'I'm a hardware store clerk,' said Miss Hughes,
'But some kinds of work I refuse.
   I'll handle their nuts,
    Their bolts and crosscuts,
But I simply will not hand out screws.'

6

A reckless young man from Fort Blaney
Made love to a spinster named Janie.
   When his friends said, 'Oh dear,
    She's so old and so queer,'
He replied, 'But the day was *so* rainy.'

7

There was a young lady of Pecking
Who indulged in a great deal of necking;
   This seemed a great waste
    Since she claimed to be chaste;
This statement, however, needs checking.

8

There was an old maid, name of Rood,
Who was such an absolute prude,
   That she pulled down the blind
    When changing her mind
Lest libidinous eyes should intrude.

9

An erstwhile old maid of Vancouver
Caught her man by an artful manoeuvre;
   For she jumped on his knee
    As he dozed by the sea.
Now, nothing on earth can remove her.

10

A spinster who came from the Ruhr
Was grasped by a vulgar young boor.
  This detestable varmint
  Unfastened her garment,
But proved to be just a voyeur.

11

There was an old lady of Harrow
Whose views were exceedingly narrow;
  At the end of her paths,
  She built two bird baths –
For the different sexes of sparrow.

12

You may not believe me, and yet,
Old girls are the very best bet.
  They don't yell, tell or swell,
  And they screw hard as hell
For it may be the last one they'll get!

13

A desperate spinster from Clare
Once knelt in the moonlight all bare,
  And prayed to her God
  For a romp on the sod –
A passer-by answered her prayer.

14

The first time she saw a man nude,
Said a diffident lady named Wood:
  'I'm glad I'm the sex
  That's concave, not convex;
For I don't fancy things that protrude.'

15

When he raped an old maid on the train,
They arrested a fellow named Braine.
   But the ex-virgin cried,
    'That's for me to decide,
And I'd be the last to complain!'

16

What he asked for (a four-letter word),
Badly frightened the virgin Miss Byrd.
   But gin and insistence
    Wore down her resistance.
The four-letter word then occurred.

17

An old maid in the land of Aloha
Got wrapped in the coils of a boa
   And, as the snake squeezed,
    The old maid, not displeased,
Cried, 'Darling! I love it! Samoa.'

18

There was an old spinster from Fife
Who had never been kissed in her life;
   Along came a cat
    And she said, 'I'll kiss that,'
But the cat meowed, 'Not on your life!'

19

Two middle-aged ladies from Fordham
Went out for a walk, and it bored 'em.
   As they made their way back,
    A sex maniac
Leapt out from the woods, and ignored 'em.

20

A lady from far Madagascar
Consented to marry a Lascar.
  Her friends thought 'twas naughty,
  But she was past forty,
And he was the first man to ask her.

21

An amorous maiden antique
Locked a man in her house for a week;
  He entered her door
  With a shout and a roar
But his exit was marked by a squeak.

22

There was an old maid of Duluth
Who wept when she thought of her youth,
  And the glorious chances
  She'd missed at school dances;
And once in a telephone booth.

23

A lonely old maid named Loretta
Sent herself an anonymous letter,
  Quoting Ellis on sex,
  And *Oedipus Rex*,
And exclaimed: 'I already feel better.'

24

A homely old spinster of France,
Who all the men looked at askance,
  Threw her skirt overhead
  And then jumped into bed
Saying, 'Now I've at least half a chance.'

25

A prudish old lady called Muir
Had a mind so incredibly pure
   That she fainted away
   At a friend's house one day
At the sight of a canary's manure.

26

A rapist, who reeked of cheap booze,
Attempted to ravish Miss Hughes;
   She cried: 'I suppose
   There's no time for my clothes,
But PLEASE let me take off my shoes!'

27

The drawers of a spinster from Lavenham
Had rude lim'ricks embroidered in Slav on 'em.
   To her lawyer she said,
   'Burn them all, when I'm dead:
For I'm damned if my nephew is having 'em.'

28

No one can tell about Myrtle
Whether she's sterile or fertile.
   If anyone tries
   To tickle her thighs
She closes them tight like a turtle.

29

A pert miss named Mary Contrary
Was attacked by a man on a ferry.
   When he'd done he said, 'Come
   On now, swallow my scum!'
'I won't – but I want to,' said Mary.

30

A young lady sat on a quay,
Just as proper as proper could be,
  A young fellow goosed her
  And roughly seduced her,
So she thanked him and went home to tea.

31

A certain young lass of Algeria
Was reduced to loud wails of hysteria
  When her escort one night
  Said, 'No, miss, honour bright,
My motives are just not ulterior!'

32

In my sweet little Alice Blue gown
I was for the first time laid down,
  I was both proud and shy
  As he opened his fly,
And the moment I saw it I thought I would die.

Oh, it hung almost down to the ground,
As it went in I made not a sound,
  The more that he shoved it
  The more that I loved it,
As he came on my Alice Blue gown.

33

A young baseball-fan named Miss Glend
Was the home-team's best rooter and friend,
  But for her the big league
  Never held the intrigue
Of a bat with two balls at the end.

34

In my sweet little nightgown of blue,
On the first night that I slept with you,
　　I was both shy and scared
　　As the bed was prepared,
And you played peekaboo with my ribbons of
　　blue.

As we both watched the break of the day,
And in peaceful submission I lay,
　　You said you adored it
　　But, dammit, you'd torn it,
My sweet little nightgown of blue.

35

There was a marine on Palau
Who looked for a girl to deflower.
　　But to his surprise
　　The Jap girls run sidewise –
To deflower on Palau takes know-how.

36

Of her 'opening night' near Fort Bliss
She explained, 'It began with a kiss,
　　And ended in bed
　　With a torn maidenhead
And my eyeballs both rolling like THIS!'

37

A naïve young lady of Bude
Had not seen a man in the nude;
　　When a lewd fellow showed
　　His all in the road,
She did not know what to conclude.

38

An astonished ex-virgin named Howard
Remarked, after being deflowered,
   'I knew that connection
   Was made in that section,
But not that it's so darn high-powered.'

39

There was a young bride named LaVerne
Who found she'd a great deal to learn:
   The man she had wed
   Took young boys into bed
And she didn't know which way to turn.

40

An unfortunate maiden was Esther;
A peculiar repugnance possessed her.
   A reaction compulsive
   Made kissing repulsive;
Which was rough on all those who caressed her.

41

On Matilda's white bosom there leaned
The cheek of a low-minded fiend,
   But she yanked up his head
   And sarcastically said,
'My boy! Won't you ever be weaned?'

42

There was a young girl from Samoa
Who said to a sailor named Noah,
   'You can kiss me and squeeze me,
   But remember, to please me,
I'm allergic to spermatozoa.'

43

There was a young lady of Gloucester
Whose friends they thought they had lost her,
   Till they found on the grass
   The marks of her arse,
And the knees of the man who had crossed her.

44

Love letters no longer they write us,
To their homes they so seldom invite us.
   It grieves me to say,
   They have learned with dismay,
We can't cure their *vulva pruritus*.

45

There once was a maid in Duluth,
A striver and seeker of truth
   This pretty wench
   Was adept at French,
And said all else was uncouth.

46

There was a young girl from Ottoreber,
Who thought young men waved their cocks at her.
   A grievous mistake
   For a young girl to make,
For they actually waved their bollocks at her.

47

There were two young ladies of Grimsby,
Who said, 'What use can our quims be?
   We know that we piddle
   Through the hole in the middle
But what use can the hairs on the rims be?'

48

When a certain young woman named Terry
Got drunk on a small sip of sherry,
   She'd insist upon games
   With embarrassing names
Not in any refined dictionary.

49

There were once two young people of taste,
Who were beautiful down to the waist;
   So they limited love
   To the regions above,
And thus remained perfectly chaste.

50

There was a young maid of Ostend,
Who swore she'd hold out to the end;
   But alas, half way over,
   'Twixt Calais and Dover
She'd done what she didn't intend.

51

There was a young person named May,
Who never let men have their way.
   But one brawny young spark
   One night in the park . . .
Now she goes to the park every day.

52

There was a young lady called Wilde
Who kept herself quite undefiled
   By thinking of Jesus,
   Contagious diseases,
And the bother of having a child.

53

There was a young girl from Bordeaux
Whose mother said, 'Always say "No".'
   But the girl said 'No' after
   The fun when, with laughter,
She'd screwed her good friend Pierrot.

54

An uptight young lady named Brearley
Who valued her morals too dearly
   Had sex, so I hear,
   Only once every year,
Which strained her pudenda severely.

55

'Yes, of course,' said a girl from Latrop,
'But it's hard to know quite where to stop:
   A boy lifts your slip
   Then you hear him unzip,
Then what do you do? Call a cop?'

56

A candid young girl named McMillan
Replied to an arrogant villain
   Who leered, 'Now I'll rape you!'
   'I cannot escape you;
But rape me you'll not, for I'm willin'.'

57

A gorgeous voluptuous creature
Seduced a young Methodist preacher;
   It worked out quite well,
   For under his spell
This gal's now a Sunday-school teacher.

58

There was a young maid of Peru,
Who swore she never would screw –
   Except under stress
   Or forceful duress,
Like: 'I'm ready. How about you?'

59

A lisping young lady called Beth
Was saved from a fate worse than death
   Seven times in a row,
   Which unsettled her so,
That she stopped saying 'No' and said 'Yeth.'

60

A prudish young girl of St Paul
Dreamt she'd undressed in the Mall.
   The best of the joke
   Was when she awoke,
And found mud on her backside and all.

61

There was a young writer named Smith,
Whose virtue was largely a myth.
   We knew how he did it:
   He couldn't have hid it –
The question was only who with.

62

There was a young lady named Smith,
Whose virtue was mostly a myth.
   She said, 'Try as I can,
   I can't find a man
Who it's fun to be virtuous with.'

63

On a blind date, the flirty Miss Rowe,
When asked for a fuck, answered, 'No!
   You can go second class
   (Shove your prick up my arse),
But I'm saving my cunt for my beau.'

64

There was a young girl called Bianca,
Who slept while her ship lay at anchor;
   She awoke with dismay,
   When she heard the mate say:
'Hi! Hoist up the top sheet and spanker!'

65

There's a very prim girl called McDrood;
What a combo – both nympho and prude!
   She wears her dark glasses
   When fellows make passes,
And keeps her eyes shut when she's screwed.

66

A boy scout was having his fill
Of a brownie's sweet charms up a hill.
   'We're prepared; yes, of course,'
   Said scoutmistress Gorse,
'My girl scouts are all on the pill.'

67

There was a young lady of Sark
Who would only make love in the dark.
   But her boyfriend said, 'Hon,
   Could you loosen your bun?
I can't tell if I'm hitting the mark.'

68

When her daughter got married in Bicester,
Her mother remarked as she kissed her,
   'That fellow you've won
   Is sure to be fun:
Since tea he's kissed me and your sister!'

69

A young woman got married in Chester,
Her mother she kissed and she blessed her.
   Says she, 'You're in luck,
   He's a stunning good fuck,
For I've had him myself down in Leicester.'

70

There was a young lady of Dee
Who went down to the river to pee.
   A man in a punt
   Put his hand on her cunt,
And God! how I wish it was me.

71

There was a young lady of Gloucester,
Met a passionate fellow who tossed her.
   She wasn't much hurt,
   But he dirtied her skirt,
So think of the anguish it cost her.

72

There was a young girl of Ostend
Who her maidenhead tried to defend.
   But a *Chasseur d'Afrique*
   Inserted his prick
And taught that ex-maid how to spend.

73

There was a young lady of Harwich
Who said on the morn of her marriage,
　'I shall sew my chemise
　Right down to my knees,
For I'm damned if I fuck in the carriage!'

74

A girl who lived in Kentucky
Said, 'Yes, I've been awfully lucky.
　No man ever yet
　On my back made me get,
But sometimes I feel awful fucky.'

75

There was a young girl of East Lynne
Whose mother, to save her from sin,
　Had filled up her crack
　To the brim with shellac,
But the boys picked it out with a pin.

76

There was a young girl of Samoa.
Who determined that no one should know her.
　One young fellow tried,
　But she wriggled aside,
And spilled all the spermatozoa.

77

There was a young lady of Kent
Who said that she knew what it meant
　When men asked her to dine,
　Gave her cocktails, and wine;
She knew what it meant: but she went!

78

Remember that maiden of Kent
Who asserted she knew what it meant
    When invited to dine
    By men who bought wine,
And went, with transparent intent?

Alas, events sometimes conspired
Not to turn out the way she desired.
    One Belgian from Ghent
    Was undoubtedly bent,
And he didn't advance, he retired.

79

There once was a lady who'd sinned,
Who said, as her abdomen thinned,
    'By my unsullied honour,
    I'm not a Madonna!
My baby has gone with the wind.'

80

There was a pure lady of Thame
Who resolved to live quite free of blame.
    She wore four pairs of drawers
    And of petticoats, scores,
But was screwed in the end, just the same.

It occurred when she crossed the Atlantic,
But the screw made young Mamie half frantic;
    It wasn't losing her cherry
    That upset her – not very,
But the aisle of a plane's *not romantic*.

Yes, he screwed her, but under great tension,
'Twas done with severe apprehension.
   She possessed (to be blunt)
   A true Klein-bottle cunt.
His prick's now in another dimension.

81

A maiden who wrote of big cities
Some songs full of love, fun and pities,
   Sold her stuff at the shop
   Of a musical wop
Who played with her soft little titties.

82

A mixed-up young person from Texas
Was full of syndromes and complexes.
   So they sent her to college
   In search of pure knowledge,
And to locate herself in the sexes.

83

C. Brontë said, 'Well, sister! What a man!
He placed me face down on the ottoman
   (Now don't you and Emily
   Go telling the femily)
And smacked me upon my bare bottom, Anne!'

84

'Watch out!' warned a mother in France,
'Let his hand reach the fuzz in your pants,
   Whilst his other hot mitt
   Is massaging your tit,
And your maidenhood won't stand a chance!'

85

Arabella's a terrible prude.
She says, 'Men are beasts. Men are lewd.
   A girl has to watch
   Or their hand's in her crotch,
And the next thing she knows, she is screwed.'

86

There are those who profess honest doubt
At your claims to be virgin, Miss Stout.
   You refuse men your cunt,
   But if I may be blunt,
Your arsehole is almost wore out.

87

It always delights me at Frank's
To walk on the old river banks.
   One time in the grass
   I stepped on an ass,
And heard a young girl murmur, 'Thanks!'

88

There was a young lass of Johore
Who was courted by gallants galore.
   Their ardent protesting
   She found interesting
And ended her life as a virgin.

89

'My dear, you've been kissing young Fred,'
A much worried mother once said,
   'Since six; it's now ten.
   Do it just once again
And then think of going to bed.'

90

Said an innocent girlie named Shelley
As her man rolled her on to her belly:
    'This is not the position
    For human coition
And why the petroleum jelly?'

91

A coon who was out with his Liz
Said, 'Baby, let's get down to biz.'
    Said she, 'That cain't be,
    Less you'se stronger'n me,
But, honey, I reckon you is.'

92

Shed a tear for the WREN named McGinnis,
Who brought her career to a finis;
    She did not understand
    The sudden command
To break out the Admiral's pinnace.

93

A girl who would not be disgraced,
Would flee from all lovers in haste.
    It all went quite well
    Till one day she fell . . .
She sometimes still dreams she is chaste.

94

A lovely young girl named Ann Heuser
Declared that no man could surprise her.
    But a fellow named Gibbons
    Untied her Blue Ribbons
And now she is sadder Budweiser

95

There was a young lady of Slough
Who said that she didn't know how –
　　Till a young fellow caught her
　　And jolly well taught her,
And she lodges in Pimlico now.

96

'It's Pony Express,' said Miss Pound:
'A wonderful game that we've found;
　　Like Post Office,' she said,
　　'But you play it in bed,
And there's a little more horsing around.'

97

When Carol was told about sex
She said, 'Mother, it sounds so complex.
　　Do you mean you and father
　　Went through all that bother,
And I'm just the after-effects?'

98

An inquisitive virgin named Dora
Whose boy was beginning to bore her,
　　'Do you mean birds and bees
　　Go through antics like these
To provide us with flora and fauna?'

99

An innocent bride from the mission
Remarked, on her first night's coition:
　　'What an intimate section
　　To use for connection.
And, Lord! what a silly position!'

100

A delighted, incredulous bride
Remarked to the groom at her side,
   'I never could quite
   Believe till tonight
Our anatomies would coincide!'

101

Said the newlyweds staying near Whiteley,
'We turn out the electric light nightly.
   It's best to embark
   Upon sex in the dark;
The look of the thing's so unsightly.'

102

A hesitant virgin named Mabel
Remarked, 'Though I'm not sure I'm able;
   I am willing to try,
   So where shall I lie?
On the bed or the floor or the table?'

103

To a young virgin friend said Miss James:
'Sex is The Most in fun games.
   What's pointed at you
   Ain't like on a statue,
For where marble dangles, meat aims!'

104

A young bride and groom of Australia
Remarked as they joined genitalia:
   'Though the system seems odd,
   We are thankful that God
Developed the genus Mammalia.'

105

There was a young lady called Kate
Who necked in the dark with her date;
   When asked how she fared
   She said she was scared,
But otherwise doing first-rate.

106

A clergyman's bride, very chaste,
Who wanted a child in great haste,
   Said, 'Mother, I grieve,
   I shall never conceive:
I just cannot get used to the taste.'

107

There was a young lady of Florence
Who for kissing professed great abhorrence;
   But when she'd been kissed,
   And found what she'd missed,
She wept till her tears came in torrents.

108

There's a pretty young lady named Sark,
Afraid to get laid in the dark,
   But she's often manhandled
   By the light of a candle
In the bushes of Gramercy Park.

109

In all of the Grecian metropolis
There was only one virgin – Papapoulos;
   But her cunt was all callous
   From fucking the phallus
Of a god that adorned the Acropolis.

110

A fair-haired young damsel named Grace
Thought it very, very foolish to place
    Her hand on your cock
    When it turned hard as rock,
For fear it would explode in her face.

111

There was a young girl named McKnight
Who got drunk with her boyfriend one night.
    She came to in bed
    With a split maidenhead –
That's the last time she ever was tight.

112

With her maidenhead gone with the wind,
Cried a happy ex-virgin named Lynd:
    'It makes me quite sick
    To have missed all that prick –
That thing has a darn candle skinned!'

113

A complacent old don of Divinity
Made boast of his daughter's virginity.
    They must have been dawdlin'
    Down at old Magdalen –
It couldn't have happened at Trinity.

114

A lassie from wee Ballachulish
Observed, 'Och, virginity's foolish;
    When a lad makes a try,
    To say ought but "Aye!"
Is stubborn, pig-headed, and mulish.'

115

A famous theatrical actress
Played best in the role of malefactress;
   Yet her home life was pure
   Except, to be sure,
A scandal or two just for practice.

116

There was a young lady of Lynn
Who was nothing but bones except skin;
   So she wore a false bust
   In the likewise false trust
That she looked like a lady of sin.

117

There was a young maiden from Multerry
Whose knowledge of life was desultory;
   She explained, like a sage:
   'Adolescence? The age
Between puberty and – er – adultery.'

118

Said a maid: 'I will marry for lucre.'
And her scandalised ma almost shucre;
   But when the chance came,
   And she told the old dame,
I notice she didn't rebucre.

119

There was a young girl with a bust
Which aroused a French cavalier's lust.
   She was since heard to say,
   About midnight, '*Touché!*
I didn't quite parry that thrust!'

120

A man who was crude and uncouth
Met up with a maiden named Ruth.
 But she gave him the air
 When he tried to betray 'er
One night in a telephone booth.

Seductions

❦

1

I, Caesar, when I learned of the fame
Of Cleopatra, I straightway laid claim.
   Ahead of my legions,
   I invaded her regions –
I saw, I conquered, I came.

2

Winter is here with his grouch,
The time when you sneeze and you slouch;
   You can't take your women
   Canoein' or swimmin':
But a lot can be done on a couch.

3

Said a voice from the back of the car
'Young man, I don't know who you are,
   But allow me to state,
   Though it may come too late,
I had not meant to go quite this far.'

4

At last I've seduced the au pair –
On steak and a chocolate eclair,
   Some peas and some chips,
   Three Miracle Whips
And a carafe of *vin ordinaire*!

5

A distinguished professor from Swarthmore
Had a date with a sexy young sophomore.
  As quick as a glance
  He stripped off his pants,
But he found that the sophomore'd got on more.

6

There was a young man of Atlanta,
Fell in love with a girl full of banter;
  'I should just like to see
  The man who'd make me,'
She remarked – and he made her instanter.

7

There was a young fellow named Louvies
Who tickled his girl in the boovies,
  And as she contorted,
  He looked down and snorted,
'My prick wants to get in your movies!'

8

There was a young fellow from Eno
Who said to his girl, 'Now, old Beano,
  Lift your skirt up in front
  And enlarge your old cunt,
For the size of this organ is keen-o.'

9

A certain young sheik I'm not namin'
Asked an actress he thought he was tamin',
  'Have you your maidenhead?'
  'Don't be silly!' she said,
'But I still have the box that it came in.'

10

A luscious young maiden of Siam
Remarked to her lover, young Kayyam,
　'If you take me, of course
　You must do it by force –
But, God knows, you're stronger than I am.'

11

There was a young fellow named Fred,
An adept at getting girls into bed.
　But by and large,
　He much preferred Marge,
As Marge was so easy to spread.

12

The last time I dined with the King
He did a quite curious thing:
　He sat on a stool,
　And took out his tool,
And said, 'If I play, will you sing?'

13

A rascal far gone in treachery,
Lured maids to their doom with his lechery;
　He invited them in
　For the purpose of sin,
Though he said 'twas to look at his etchery.

14

Though his plan, when he gave her a buzz,
Was to do what man normally does,
　She declared: 'I'm a Soul;
　Not a sexual goal – '
So he shrugged, and called someone who was.

15

I met a lewd nude in Bermuda
Who thought she was shrewd: I was shrewder;
    She thought it quite crude
    To be wooed in the nude.
I pursued her, subdued her, and screwed her.

16

Said a very attractive young Haitian,
'Please begin with a gentle palpation.
    If you do as I say
    In the way of foreplay'
Why, who knows? There may be fornication.'

17

A lustful old codger from Sheds
Delights to pop girls' maidenheads.
    He claims, 'Virgins long,
    Oftentimes, to go wrong
It's that first painful pop a girl dreads.'

18

On a date with a charming young bird
His erotic emotions were stirred.
    So with bold virile pluck,
    He enquired, 'Do you fuck?'
She said, 'Yes, but please don't use that word.'

19

I dislike all this crude notoriety
That I'm getting for my impropriety;
    All that I ever do
    Is what girls ask me to –
I admit, I get lots of variety.

20

There was a young lady of Glasgow,
And fondly her lover did ask, 'Oh,
　　Pray allow me a fuck,'
　　But she said, 'No, my duck,
But you may, if you please, up my arse go.'

21

An observant young man of the West
Said, 'I've found out by personal test
　　That men who make passes
　　At girls who wear glasses
Have just as good fun as the rest.'

22

Seducing shy virgins to sin
Takes more than sweet-talking and gin:
　　An all-out seduction
　　Is a major production.
It may take you days to get in.

23

For years all the young men had striven
To seduce a young lady named Ruthven;
　　Till a fellow named Bert
　　Felt his way up her skirt –
In Heaven such sins are forgiven.

24

A girl who was touring Zambesi
Said, 'Attracting the men is quite easy:
　　I don't wear any pants
　　And at every chance,
I stand where it's frightfully breezy.'

25

Said a guy to his girlfriend, 'Virginia
For ages I've courted to win ya.
   Now my point of frustration
   Has reached saturation –
This evening I gotta get in ya!'

26

The haughty philosopher Plato
Would unbend to a sweet young tomato.
   Though she might be naïve
   Like you wouldn't believe
He would patiently show her the way to.

27

I was sitting there, taking my ease
And enjoying my Beaumes-de-Venise
   With a charming young poppet,
   But she told me to stop it
As my fingers crept up past her knees.

28

Breathed a tender young man from Australia,
'My darling, please let me unveilia,
   And then, O my own,
   If you'll kindly lie prone,
I'll endeavour, my sweet, to impaleia.'

29

There was a young fellow named Harry,
Had a joint that was long, huge and scary.
   He pressed it on a virgin
   Who, without any urgin',
Immediately spread like a fairy.

30

A lad from far-off Transvaal
Was lustful, but tactful withal.
　　He'd say, just for luck,
　　'Mam'selle, do you fuck?'
But he'd bow till he almost would crawl.

31

There was a young lady of Clewer
Who was riding a bike and it threw her.
　　A man saw her there
　　With her legs in the air,
And seized the occasion to screw her.

32

A lazy, fat fellow named Betts
Upon his fat ass mostly sets.
　　Along comes a gal
　　And says, 'I'll fuck you, pal.'
Says he, 'If you'll do the work, let's.'

33

Said a naked young soldier named Mickey,
As his cunt eyed his stiff, throbbing dickey,
　　'Kid, my leave's almost up,
　　But I feel like a tup;
Bend down, and I'll slip you a quickie.'

34

A self-centred young fellow named Newcombe,
Who seduced many girls but made few come,
　　Said, 'The pleasures of tail
　　Were ordained for the male.
I've had mine. Do I care whether you come?'

35

In *La France* once a clevair young man
Met a girl on the beach down at Cannes.
    Said the mademoiselle,
    'Eh, m'sieu, vot ze 'ell?
Stay away where eet ees not son-tan!'

36

There was a shy boy named Dan
Who tickled his girl with a fan.
    She started to flirt
    So he lifted her skirt
And gave her a flick like a man.

37

A proper young person named Gissing
Announced he had given up kissing.
    'I strike out at once
    For something that counts –
And besides, my girl's front teeth are missing.'

38

A handsome young widow named Vi
Seduced all the wardens nearby.
    When the siren said: 'Woo!'
    What else could they do
To extinguish the gleam in her eye?

Appetites and Longings

❧

1

There was a young man from Toledo
Who travelled about incognito.
   The reason he did
   Was to bolster his id
Whilst appeasing his savage libido.

2

A woman there was named Pauline
Who's always been terribly keen
   On kissing and wooing,
   Indiscriminate screwing,
And anything else that's obscene.

3

There was once a girl from Red Hook
Who said, 'Though I could be mistook,
   One more time ought to do
   To get me and you
Into Guinness's world record book.'

4

A sweet little deb named Miss Shaw
Was fucking with boys more and more;
   Knowing digital pleasure
   Was a far safer measure,
Yet, 'Hell!' she said, 'what's a cunt for?'

5

There once was a handsome young seaman
Who with ladies was really a he-man.
  In peace or in war,
  At sea or on shore,
Like a demon, he'd dish out his semen.

6

There was a young lady named Mabel
Who liked to sprawl out on the table,
  Then cry to her man
  'Stuff in all you can –
Your bollocks as well, if you're able.'

7

An insatiable satyr named Frazer
Is known as a wild woman-chaser.
  He's the main cause of myriads
  Of overdue periods
For to him 'rubber' means an eraser.

8

At the orgy I humped twenty-two,
And was glad when the whole thing was through;
  I don't find it swinging
  To do all this change-ringing,
But at orgies, what else can you do?

9

There was a sweet lassie named Harriet
Who would take on two lads in a chariot;
  Then six monks and four tailors,
  Nine priests and eight sailors,
Muhammad and Judas Iscariot.

10

There was a young Scot in Madrid
Who got fifty-five fucks for a quid.
   When they said, 'Are you faint?'
   He replied, 'No, I ain't,
But I don't feel as good as I did.'

11

The wife of an absent dragoon
Begged a soldier to grant her a boon:
   As she let down her drawers,
   She said, 'It's all yours –
I could deal with the whole damned platoon!'

12

Sweet nymphomanic Miss Stainer
Finds most male sex organs now pain her.
   'I guess that I've blundered,'
   She said. 'Seven hundred
Are too much for one small container.'

13

There is a young lady named Aird
Whose bottom is always kept bared;
   When asked why, she pouts,
   And says the boy scouts
All beg her to please be prepared!

14

There was a young lady of Bicester
Who was nicer by far than her sister:
   The sister would giggle
   And wiggle and jiggle,
But this one would come if you kissed her.

15

There was a young lady of Dover,
Whose passion was such that it drove her
    To cry, when you came,
    'Oh dear! What a shame!
Well, now we shall have to start over.'

16

There was a gay dog from Ontario
Who fancied himself a Lothario.
    At a wench's glance
    He'd snatch off his pants
And make for her mons Venerio.

17

A wanton young lady of Wimleigh
Reproached for not acting more primly,
    Answered, 'Heavens above,
    I know sex isn't love,
But it's such an attractive facsimile!'

18

There was a young woman who lay
With her legs wide apart in the hay.
    Then, calling a ploughman,
    She said: 'Do it now, man!
Don't wait till your hair has turned grey!'

19

A very smart lady named Cookie
Said, 'I like to mix gambling with nookie.
    Before every race
    I go home to my place
And curl up with a very good bookie.'

20

She wasn't what one would call pretty
And other girls offered her pity;
   So nobody guessed
   That her Wasserman test
Involved half the men in the city.

21

There was a young princess called Dagmar
Who said, 'I should so like to shag, ma.'
   And says she, 'If you speaks
   To the King of the Greeks,
He will lend me his own tolliwag, ma.'

22

'Far dearer to me than my treasure,'
The heiress declared, 'is my leisure.
   For then I can screw
   The whole Harvard crew –
They're slow, but that lengthens the pleasure.'

23

There was a young fellow named Pete
Who was gentle, and shy, and discreet;
   But with his first woman
   He became quite inhuman
And constantly roared for fresh meat.

24

Brigham Young was never a neutah,
A pansy or fairy or fruitah.
   Where ten thousand virgins
   Succumbed to his urgin's
We now have the great state of Utah.

25

There was a young couple from Florida,
Whose passion grew steadily torrider.
    They had planned to sin
    At a room in the inn.
Who can wait? So they screwed in the corridor.

26

Said a certain old earl whom I knew,
'I've been struck from the rolls of *Who's Who*,
    Just because I was found
    Lying prone on the ground
With the housemaid, and very nice too!'

27

'Gracious me,' said the Duke of Buccleuch,
'I've been struck from the rolls of *Who's Who*,
    All because I was found
    Lying nude on the ground
With my granny, and very nice, too!'

28

To his nurse said the famous physician,
In the throes of illicit coition:
    'Though it's getting quite late
    Let the damn patients wait!
Please assume the *post-partum* position.'

29

There was a young fellow called Lancelot,
Whom his neighbours all looked on askance a lot:
    Whenever he'd pass
    A presentable lass,
The front of his pants would advance a lot.

30

There was a young fellow named Charteris
Put his hand where his young lady's garter is.
   Said she, 'I don't mind,
   And up higher you'll find
The place where my fucker and farter is.'

31

Said a virile young tourist from Galion
Who was hung like a champion stallion:
   'I've fucked girls from Fort Worth
   To the ends of the earth –
None better the female Italian.'

32

There is something about satyriasis
That arouses psychiatrists' biases.
   But we're both very pleased
   We're in this way diseased
As the damsel who's waiting to try us is.

33

Down in Rome, Washburn Child,
A lecherous fellow and wild –
   Like his buddy, King Vic,
   He likes thrusting his prick
Into twats hitherto undefiled.

34

The French are a race among races;
They fuck in the funniest places:
   Any orifice handy
   Is thought to be dandy
Including the one in their faces.

35

Here's to it, and through it, and to it again,
To suck it, and screw it, and screw it again!
　　So in with it, out with it,
　　Lord work his will with it!
Never a day we don't do it again!

36

There are three ladies of Huxham
And whenever we meets 'em we fucks 'em,
　　And when that game grows stale
　　We sits on a rail
And pulls out our pricks and they sucks 'em.

37

There once was a Hun, named Attila,
Whose life was a genuine thrilla.
　　From village to village
　　He'd rant, rape and pillage,
Seldom spending two nights on one pilla.

His neighbours objected, it's true,
To the way he would plunder and screw.
　　But he'd say, ' 'Tain't my fault,
　　'Cause it's all the resault
Of a trauma I suffered at two.'

38

On an outing with seventeen Czechs,
A girl tourist supplied the free sex.
　　She returned from the jaunt
　　Feeling more or less gaunt,
But the Czechs were all absolute wrecks.

39

A haughty young wench of Del Norte
Would fuck only men over forty.
   Said she, 'It's too quick
   With a young fellow's prick;
I like it to last, and be warty.'

40

The orgy was held on the lawn,
And we knocked off two hours before dawn.
   We found ourselves viewing
   Twenty-two couples screwing,
But by sun-up they'd all come and gone.

41

A young man by a girl was desired
To give her the thrills she required;
   But he died of old age
   Ere his cock could assuage
The volcanic desires it inspired.

42

There was a young bride named McWing
Who thought sex a delirious fling.
   When her bridegroom grew ill
   From too much (as they will),
She found other men do the same thing.

43

There was a young lady called Maud,
A sort of society fraud;
   In the parlour, 'tis told,
   She was distant and cold,
But on the verandah, my Gawd!

44

There was a young wife from Peoria
Who checked into the Waldorf Astoria
   Where she stayed for a week
   With two Swedes and a Greek
In a state of near-total euphoria.

45

There was a young girl named Priscilla
With whom sex proved completely a thriller.
   One just can't get enough
   Of that girl's kind of stuff
Although the sixth time it's a killer.

46

The enjoyment of sex, although great,
Is in later years said to abate.
   This well may be so,
   I'm afraid I don't know,
For I'm now only seventy-eight.

47

When Cupid loved Psyche, it seems
That their sex-life was one of extremes.
   Their performance in bed
   Exceeded, it's said,
The wildest sex orgies of dreams.

48

Beryl's face appears careworn and ashen,
And it's all due to sexual passion.
   Though it's turning her grey,
   She 'makes love' night and day
As though it might go out of fashion.

49

There was a young man of Eau Claire
Enjoying his girl on the stair.
 At the forty-fourth stroke
 The bannister broke,
And he finished her off in mid-air.

50

A comely young widow named Ransom
Was ravished three times in a hansom.
 When she cried out for more
 A voice from the floor
Said, 'Madam, I'm Simpson, not Samson.'

51

There was a young lady from Putney
Who was given to sexual gluttony.
 Warned a pious old duffer
 'Your morals will suffer.'
'That's what you think,' she said. 'I ain't got any.'

52

My boy, if you like to have fun;
If you take all the girls one by one.
 And when reaching four score
 Still don't find it a bore
Why then, you're a hero, my son.

53

Have you heard of the boxer named Jules
Whose hunger for sex never cools?
 He pays no attention
 To social convention
Or the Marquis of Queensberry's rules.

54

Said Queen Isabella of Spain,
'I like it now and again.
    But I wish to explain
    That by "now and again'
I mean now and again and AGAIN.'

55

'It is no use,' said Lady Maude Hoare,
    'I can't concentrate any more.
    You're all in a sweat,
    And the sheets are quite wet,
And just look at the time: half-past four!'

56

There was a young man from the War Office
Who got into bed with a whore of his.
    She slipped off her drawers
    With many a pause
But the chap from the War Office tore off his.

57

There's an over-sexed lady named White
Who insists on a dozen a night.
    A fellow named Cheddar
    Had the brashness to wed her –
His chance of survival is slight.

58

'Austerity now is the fashion,'
Remarked a young lady with passion.
    Then she glanced at the bed
    And quietly said,
'But there's one thing that no one can ration.'

59

There was a young lady of fashion,
Who had oodles and oodles of passion;
 To her lover she said,
 As they climbed into bed:
'Here's one thing the bastards can't ration.'

60

There was a young fellow in Maine
Who courted a girl all in vain;
 She cussed when he kissed her
 So he slept with her sister
Again and *again* and AGAIN.

61

There was a young lady of Lynn
Who was deep in original sin;
 When they said, 'Do be good!'
 She said, 'Would if I could!'
And straightway went at it again.

62

There was a young woman of Dee,
Who stayed with each man she did see;
 When it came to the rest,
 She wished to be best,
And practice makes perfect you see.

63

Said Miss Farrow, on one of her larks,
'Sex is more fun in bed than in parks.
 You feel more at ease;
 Your butt doesn't freeze
And passers-by don't make remarks.'

64

While the Prof wrote a Latin declension,
His pupils did things one can't mention,
Like screwing and blowing
Each other, and showing
A singular lack of attention.

65

Cleopatra, when sex was still new to her,
Kept buying up young slaves to tutor her.
But the Pharaoh (her dad)
For fear she'd go bad
Kept rendering them neuterer and neuterer.

66

There was a young fellow of Tulsa
Who said, 'Sex has grown very dull, sir.
Yet I'm that much a dope,
If a girl says there's hope,
I don't have the heart to repulse her.'

67

There once was a lady named Mabel,
So ready, so willing, so able,
And so full of spice
She could name her own price –
Now Mabel's all wrapped up in sable.

68

There once was a husky young Viking
Whose sexual prowess was striking.
Every time he got hot
He would scour the twat
Of some girl that might be to his liking.

69

The wife of a chronic crusader
Took on every man who waylaid her.
 Till the amorous itch
 Of this popular bitch
So annoyed the crusader he spayed her.

70

If you're speaking of actions immoral,
Then how about giving the laurel
 To doughty Queen Esther?
 No three men could best her –
One fore and one aft and one oral.

71

There once was a fellow named Abbott
Who made love to girls as a habit;
 But he ran for the door
 When one girl asked for more,
And exclaimed, 'I'm a man, not a rabbit.'

72

It was on the 7th of December
That Franklin D. took out his member.
 He said, like the bard,
 'It will be long and very hard,
Pearl Harbor has given me something to remember.'

73

Girls give Jim's stiff penis a spasm
Whenever he sees 'em or has 'em.
 He likes them so well
 He needs only to smell
Them, to have a spontaneous orgasm.

74

There was a young lady named Duff
With a lovely, luxuriant muff.
  In his haste to get in her
  One eager beginner
Lost both of his balls in the rough.

75

A highly bored damsel called Brown,
Remarked as she laid herself down:
  'I hate to be doing
  This promiscuous screwing,
But what else can you *do* in this town?'

76

There was a young lady named Moore
Who, while not quite precisely a whore,
  Couldn't pass up a chance
  To take down her pants
And compare some man's stroke with her bore.

77

That man is undoubtedly rare
Who can stare at a bare *derrière*
  And be so unimpressed
  By Sweet Fanny, undressed,
That his flag doesn't wave in the air.

Thrills

❦

1

There was a young student named Jones
Who'd reduce any maiden to moans
   By his wonderful knowledge,
   Acquired in college,
Of nineteen erogenous zones.

2

There was a young fellow named Meek
Who perfected a lingual technique.
   It drove women frantic
   But (much less romantic)
It chafed all the skin off his cheek.

3

There was a young plumber of Leigh
Who was plumbing a maid by the sea.
   Said the maid, 'Cease your plumbing:
   I think someone's coming!'
Said the plumber, still plumbing, 'It's me!'

4

The sex-drive of old man McGill
Gives fortunate ladies a thrill.
   They say his technique
   Is delightful, unique:
And involves an electrical drill!

5

I kissed her red lips with intention
Of proceeding to things I won't mention.
  Now, who could suppose
  That her pretty pink toes
Would grip on to my virile extension!

6

There was a young lady of Fez
Who was known to the public as 'Jez'.
  Jezebel was her name,
  Sucking cocks was the game
She excelled at, so everyone says.

7

A tidy young lady named Streeter
Loved dearly to nibble a peter.
  And always she'd say,
  'I prefer it this way.
I think it is very much neater.'

8

None could better our sex limousine
With its neat, built-in fucking machine.
  Engine-powered, this connects
  To suit either sex,
And adjusts to the fat and the lean.

9

'Of course,' said the Prince Paletine,
'I agree fornication is fine,
  But I entertain 'em
  Per os et per anum,
Which last I consider divine!'

10

There was a young maiden named Rose
With erogenous zones in her toes.
   She remained onanistic
   Till a foot-fetishistic
Young man became one of her beaus.

11

A prosperous merchant of Rhone
Fills sexual orders by phone,
   Or the same can be baled,
   Stamped, labelled and mailed
To a limited parcel-post zone.

12

There was an old lady of Troy
Who invented a new sort of joy:
   She sugared her quim
   And frosted the rim,
And then had it sucked by a boy.

13

There was a young miss from Johore
Who'd lie on a mat on the floor,
   In a manner uncanny
   She'd wriggle her fanny,
And drain your nuts dry to the core.

14

A candid young lady named Tudor
Remarked to the chap who'd just screwed her,
   'After dildoes, dilators,
   And electric vibrators,
The real thing feels like an intruder.'

15

Some night when you're drunk on Dutch Bols
Try changing the usual roles.
    The backward position
    Is nice for coition
And offers the choice of two holes.

16

I know of a fortunate Hindu
Who is sought in the towns that he's been to,
    By the ladies he knows
    Who are thrilled to the toes
By the tricks he can make his foreskin do.

17

There was a young lady of Brussels
Whose pride was her vaginal muscles;
    She could easily plex them
    And so interflex them
As to whistle love songs through her bustles.

18

According to old Sigmund Freud,
Life is seldom so well enjoyed
    As in human coition
    (In any position)
With the usual organs employed.

19

A vibrant and virile young Viking
For intercourse had a great liking.
    He would shatter the asses
    Of sweet Viking lasses
Resembling ball-lightning striking.

20

An Australian fellow named Menzies
By kissing sent girls into frenzies.
   But a virgin one night
   Crossed her legs in a fright
And shattered his bifocal lenses.

21

With his penis in turgid erection,
And aimed at woman's mid-section,
   Man looks most uncouth
   In that moment of truth
But she sheathes it with loving affection.

22

There was a young man from Winsocket
Who put a girl's hand in his pocket.
   Her delicate touch
   Thrilled his pecker so much,
It shot off in the air like a rocket.

23

There was two Greek girls of Miletus
Who said, 'We wear gadgets that treat us,
   When strapped on the thigh
   Up cozy and high,
To constant, convenient coitus.'

24

At Vassar sex isn't injurious
Though of love we are never penurious.
   Thanks to vulcanized aids
   Though we may die old maids
At least we shall never die curious.

25

A cheerful old party of Lucknow
Remarked, 'I should just like a fuck now!'
   So he had one and spent
   And said, 'I'm content.
By no means am I so cunt-struck now.'

26

There was a young girl of Darjeeling,
Who danced with such exquisite feeling;
   There was never a sound
   For miles around,
Save of fly-buttons hitting the ceiling.

27

A book and a jug and a dame,
And a nice cosy nook for the same.
   'And I don't care a damn,'
   Said Omar Khayyam,
'What you say. It's a great little game.'

28

There was a young lady from Munich
Who had an affair with a eunuch.
   At the height of their passion
   He dealt her a ration
From a squirt gun concealed in his tunic.

29

'Near my girl' said a lecher named Cecil,
'Is the place where I usually nestle.
   Nothing else is a patch
   On the way that we match:
She's the mortar and I am the pestle.'

30

A lonely young fellow of Eton
Used always to sleep with the heat on,
    Till he met a young lass,
    Who showed him her ass –
Now they're sleeping with only a sheet on.

31

A plumber from Lowater Creek
Was called in by a dame with a leak.
    She looked so becoming
    He fixed all her plumbing
And didn't emerge for a week.

32

'Last night,' said a lassie named Ruth,
'In a long-distance telephone booth,
    I enjoyed the perfection
    Of an ideal connection –
I was screwed, if you must know the truth.'

33

There was a young man named Racine,
Who invented a fucking machine:
    Concave and convex,
    It would fit either sex,
With attractions for those in between.

34

There was a young lady named Gay
Who was asked to make love in the hay.
    She jumped at the chance
    And took off her pants:
She was tickled to try it that way.

35

A responsive young girl from the East
In bed was an able artiste.
 She had learned two positions
 From family physicians,
And ten more from the old parish priest.

36

There was a young girl of Detroit,
Who at fucking was very adroit.
 She could squeeze her vagina
 To a pin-point and finer,
Or open it out like a quoit.

37

There was a young man of Dumfries
Who said to his girl, 'If you please,
 It would give me great bliss
 If while playing with this
You would give some attention to these.'

38

That super-hot satyr named Rex
Is an absolute master of sex:
 With his hot hairy hands
 Massaging girls' glands,
Causing all the expected effects.

39

There was a young monarch called Ed
Who took Mrs Simpson to bed!
 As they bounced up and down
 He said, 'Bugger the Crown!
We'll give it to Bertie instead.'

40

Old Louis Quatorze was hot stuff.
He tired of that game, blind man's buff;
   Upended his mistress,
   Kissed hers, while she kissed his,
And thus taught the world *soixante-neuf*.

41

There was a young man from Oswego
Who fell in love with a dago.
   He dreamt that his Venus
   Was jerking his penis
And woke up all covered with sago.

42

Of his face she thought *not* very much,
But then, at the very first touch,
   Her attitude shifted –
   He was terribly gifted
At frigging and fucking and such.

43

There was a young man in Schenectady,
And he found it quite hard to erect, said he,
   Till he took an injection
   For deficient erection,
Which in just the desired way affected he!

44

There was a young man named Walljasper
Who invented a fur-lined ball-clasper.
   A half turn to the right
   Would bring squeals of delight
To the most sterile, im*po*tent whoremaster.

45

A certain young fellow named Dick
Liked to feel a girl's hand on his prick.
    He taught them to fool
    With his rigid old tool
Till the cream shot out, white and thick.

46

An agreeable girl named Miss Doves
Likes to jack off the young men she loves.
    She will use her bare fist
    If the fellows insist
But she really prefers to wear gloves.

47

There was a young lady of Dallas
Invented a singular phallus.
    It came and it went,
    And when it was spent
It proceeded to fill up the chalice

48

The team of Tom and Louise
Do an act in the nude on their knees.
    They crawl down the aisle
    While screwing dog-style
And the orchestra plays Kilmer's *Trees*.

49

There was once a mechanic named Bench
Whose best tool was a sturdy gut-wrench.
    With this vibrant device
    He could reach, in a trice,
The innermost parts of a wench.

50

A young window-cleaner named Luigi
Was screwing a lady from Fiji.
    When she broke into sweat
    He said, 'Hold on, my pet,'
And squeezed off the sweat with his squeegee.

51

There once was a dentist named Stone
Who saw all his patients alone.
    In a fit of depravity
    He filled the wrong cavity,
And my! how his practice has grown!

52

The cute little schoolteacher said,
As she gleefully hopped into bed:
    'If the lads and the lasses
    In my hygiene classes
Could see me right now, they'd drop dead!'

53

A buxom young beauty named Beulah
Each night entertained with a hula:
    'Twas rather *risqué*
    In a mild sort of way,
But she made quite a bundle of moula.

54

There was a young lady of Wheeling
Who professed to lack sexual feeling.
    But a cynic named Boris
    Just touched her clitoris
And she had to be scraped off the ceiling.

55

A young man of Novorossisk
Had a mating procedure so brisk,
　　With such super-speed action,
　　The Lorentz contraction
Foreshortened his prick to a disk.

56

There was a young man from McGill
Who was always seen walking uphill.
　　When someone enquired,
　　'My man, aren't you tired?'
He said, 'No, it make my balls thrill.'

57

In the quaint English village of Worcester
Lived a little red hen and a rooster.
　　A coquettish glance
　　She acquired in France
Gave him ants in his pants, and he goosed her.

58

The favourite pastime of grandfather
Was tickling his balls with a feather.
　　But the thing he liked best
　　Of all the rest
Was knocking them gently together.

59

The Duchess of Drood's lewd and crude,
And the men think her terribly rude.
　　When they swim by the docks,
　　She tickles their cocks
And laughs when the red tips protrude.

60

There was a young girl, very sweet,
Who thought sailors' meat quite a treat.
　　When she sat on their lap
　　She unbuttoned their flap,
And always had plenty to eat.

61

A company of Grenadier Guards
While traversing the park, formed in squads,
　　Saw two naked statues
　　At three-quarter pratt views,
Which perceptibly stiffened their rods.

62

A once-famous gatherer of leeches
Has taken to combing the beaches,
　　Where he helps all the aunties
　　On and off with their panties,
And they help him off with his breeches.

63

There was a young girlie named Hannah
Who loved madly her lover's banana.
　　She loved pubic hair
　　And balls that were bare,
And she jacked him off in her bandanna.

64

There was a young girl of Moline
Whose fucking was sweet and obscene.
　　She would work on a prick
　　With every known trick,
And finish by winking it clean.

65

A fanatic gun-lover named Crust
Was perverse to the point of disgust:
    His idea of a peach
    Had a sixteen-inch breech
And a pearl-handled .44 bust.

66

A eunuch who came from Port Said
Had a jolly good time in bed,
    Nor could any sultana
    Detect from his manner
That he used a banana instead.

67

There once was a lady from Arden
Who sucked off a man in a garden.
    He said, 'My dear Flo,
    Where does all that stuff go?'
And she said – swallowing hard – 'I beg pardon?'

Trollops and Tarts

1

There was a young lady of Norwood
Whose ways were provokingly forward.
   Her mother said, 'Dear,
   Please don't wriggle your rear
Like a trollop or tart or a whore would.'

2

A modern young girl from Eau Claire
Remarked, as she sprawled in a chair,
   'I can tell from your glance
   I forgot to wear pants;
So stare at my crotch – I don't care!'

3

'I just can't be bothered with drawers,'
Said one of our better-known whores.
   'There isn't much doubt
   I do better without
In handling my everynight chores.'

4

There is a young woman from Venice –
A regular sexual menace –
   For she'll hop from one boy
   To another with joy,
Like the ball in a fast game of tennis.

5

Antoinette was a beautiful whore
Who wore fifty-six beads – nothing more.
   They sneered 'Unrefined'
   When she wore them behind,
So she tactfully wore them before.

6

A charmer from old Amarillo,
Sick of finding strange heads on her pillow,
   Decided one day
   That to keep them away
She would plug up her crevice with Brillo.

7

There was a young harlot from Kew
Who filled her vagina with glue.
   Said she, with a grin,
   'If they pay to get in,
They'll pay to get out of it, too.'

8

Come to Noah's for wine and strong waters,
And for screwing in clean classy quarters.
   I assure every guest
   I've made personal test
Of my booze and my beds and my daughters.

9

Three whores took on nine men at once,
In their arse-holes and mouths and their cunts.
   On golf links or green
   Are more usually seen
Eighteen balls and nine holes at such stunts.

10

There was an old lady of Cheltenham
Said, 'Cunts? Why of course, dear,
   I dealt in 'em. I thought it my duty
   To make 'em so fruity
My clients used simply to melt in 'em.'

11

Nymphomaniacal Jill
Tried a dynamite stick for a thrill.
   They found her vagina
   In North Carolina
And bits of her tits in Brazil.

12

A happy young whore from Milpitas
Said, 'Man has found nothing to beat us.
   Golf, fishing and fights
   All have their delights,
But nothing beats good old coitus!'

13

Your average French girls are no ladies,
They'll do most things to get a Mercedes.
   In private or whore-office
   They peddle each orifice,
Nor care if they end up in Hades.

14

To a whore, said the cold Lady Dizzit,
'Lord D's a new man, since your visit.
   As a rule, the damned fool
   Can't erect his old tool.
You must have what it takes; but what is it?'

15

There once was a girl named McGoffin
Who was diddled amazingly often.
   She was rogered by scores
   Who'd been turned down by whores,
And was finally screwed in her coffin.

16

An elderly harlot from Trings
Has fucked the last four Spanish kings.
   Says she, 'They're all short
   And no good at the sport;
But the queen, who is Lesbian, swings.'

17

There was a young lady from Leicester
Who allowed the young men to molest her.
   For a kiss and a squeeze
   She would open her knees;
And she'd strip to the buff if they pressed her.

18

There was a debauched little wench
Whom nothing could ever make blench.
   She admitted men's poles
   At all possible holes,
And she'd bugger, fuck, jerk-off and french.

19

There was a young harlot from Leigh
Who slipped into church for a pee.
   Without any malice
   She pissed in the chalice
While singing the *Agnus Dei*.

20

There were two young men of Cawnpore,
Who buggered and fucked the same whore.
   But the partition split,
   And the spunk and the shit
Rolled out in great lumps on the floor.

21

There was a young girl of St Cyr,
Whose reflex reactions were queer;
   Her escort said: 'Mabel!
   Get up off the table!
That money is there for the beer.'

22

Up the street sex is sold by the piece,
And I wish that foul traffic would cease;
   It's a shame and improper,
   And I'd phone for a copper
But that's where you'll find the police.

23

'Competition is keen, you'll agree,'
Said an ancient old flapper from Dee.
   So she dyed her grey tresses
   Chopped a foot from her dresses,
And her *reason* you plainly can see.

24

There was a young fellow named Dave
Who kept a dead whore in a cave.
   He said, 'I admit
   I'm a bit of a shit,
But think of the money I save!'

25

Unattractive as Mabel may be
What she has that I want, she gives free.
    The local love stores
    Charge too much for their whores,
So it's Mabel (dear Mabel) for me!

26

A naughty old colonel of Butte
Had a habit his friends thought was cutte.
    He'd slip off to Spokane
    And proceed from the train
To a house of distinct ill-reputte.

27

There was a young man of high station
Who was found by a pious relation
    Making love in a ditch
    To – I won't say a bitch –
But a woman of NO reputation.

28

Said a woman from Richmond, Virginia,
I'd be rich if I only were skinnier.
    If I lost thirty pounds
    The boys would have grounds
To say, 'How I'd pay to be in ya'.'

29

Of my clients, I like best the go-getter
Who is rich and disdains a french letter.
    Some men think a lot of me
    Who profess to like bottomy
But, for me, frontal twatomy's better.

30

You remember the whore from New York
Who stoppered her cunt with a cork?
   A woodpecker (or yaffle)
   Had a go at that baffle
But it sure put a stop to the stork;

Till along came a man who presented
A tool that was strangely indented.
   With a dizzying twirl
   He punctured that girl –
And thus was the corkscrew invented.

31

There was an old fellow of Ewing
Who said, 'It's computing I'm doing.
   By leaving my drawers on
   While clambering whores, on
The whole I've lost ten miles of screwing.'

32

I was asked by a lecher named Spicer,
'Is there anything, really, that's nicer
   Than a neat bit of crumpet
   With an amiable strumpet
Who doesn't expect you to splice her?'

33

There once was a pro from Madrid,
Whose minimum charge was a quid.
   Came along an Italian,
   With balls like a stallion,
Said he'd do it for nothing, and did.

34

Salome! Salome! Where art?
Thou biblical strip-teasing tart!
　　I'd have thought that, instead
　　Of Jokanaan's head,
Thou'd'st have asked a more pertinent part.

35

There was a young girl from Baroda
Who built an erotic pagoda.
　　The walls of its halls
　　Were festooned with the balls
And the tools of the fools who bestrode her.

36

There was a young girl of Newcastle
Whose charms were declared universal;
　　With one man in front,
　　Wired into her cunt,
And another engaged at her arsehole.

37

Said a charming young lady of Padua,
'A peso! Why, sir, what a cadua!'
　　He said, lifting his hat,
　　'You ain't even worth that.
However, I'm glad to have hadua.'

38

In Wall Street a girl named Irene
Made an offering somewhat obscene:
　　She stripped herself bare
　　And offered a share
To Merrill Lynch, Pierce, Fenner and Beane.

39

There was a young harlot of Clyde
Whose doctor cut open her hide.
   He misplaced his stitches
   And closed the wrong niches;
She now does her work on the side.

40

A pimp toured his whore through ten nations,
Selling sundry and various sexations,
   And when asked his position,
   Answered, 'Pushing coition –
I handle her pubic relations.'

41

A spritely young woman named Wise
One midsummer evening gave rise
   To a chain of events
   Involving six gents
In a general unzipping of flies.

42

A young girl was no good at tennis
But at swimming was really a 'menace';
   The cause, she explained,
   Was the way she had trained:
She had been a streetwalker in Venice.

43

A fallen young lady of fashion
Gave vent to all sorts of base passion.
   Was she scorned? She was not,
   For her ways brought a lot
Of highly respectable cash in.

44

A lazy young houri named Hayes
Said, 'I'm happy to give my guys lays
    If they bring vaseline
    Or plain margarine,
But I hate to waste good mayonnaise!'

45

The town's leading trollop, Miss Barkis,
Rents the genital parts of her carcass.
    For lust she must thank
    Daily trips to the bank
And a sable fur coat (Neiman-Marcus).

46

The chief charm of a whore in Shalott
Was the absence of hair on her twat.
    She kept it smooth-looking
    Not by shaving or plucking,
But by all of the fucking she got.

47

Said Jane, 'I just love to exhibit:
A delight I let nothing inhibit.
    I think it's a ball
    To undress and bare all –
Oh, I'm such a young flibbertigibbet!'

48

An awful old bounder, McGee,
Used to think he could dip his wick free.
    But a harlot named Charlotte
    Remarked with a snarl, 'It
Is business, not pleasure, with me.'

49

There was a young girl from the Saar
Who'd take all men, from near or from far.
   When asked to explain,
   She replied, with disdain,
'I'm working to buy a new car.'

50

A starry-eyed starlet named Charlotte
Said, 'Hollywood! Home of the harlot!
   Where cute split-tail bitches
   Take quick rides to riches,
If their sins are sufficiently scarlet.

51

A kindly old harlot from China
Declared, 'I have never felt finer;
   And so poor men won't holler,
   I'll charge just $1,
And 25¢ for a minor.'

52

There was an old madam named Rainey
Adept at her business, and brainy.
   She charged ten bucks or more
   For a seasoned old whore,
But a dollar would get you a trainee.

53

There's a luscious young charmer named Carmen
Who fucks for bums, boxers and barmen.
   Says she, 'The effete
   Have more brains but less meat.
I prefer hairy fellows who *are* men!'

54

A sweet Georgia peach of high station
Became overnight a sensation,
   When she took on Fort Benning
   And charged not a pfennig,
Saying, 'Who could do less for her nation?'

55

A guy met a girl in Anacostia
And said, 'Darling, dare I accost ya?
   I've got only a buck,
   Is that good for a fuck?'
She replied, 'Not a fart will it cost ya.'

56

A much-diddled dolly named Beverley
Goes about her sex bouts so darned cleverly,
   She services three
   At a time – all for free –
Positioned about herself severally.

57

A notorious whore named Miss Hearst
In the weakness of men is well-versed.
   Reads a sign over the head
   Of her well-rumpled bed:
'The customer always comes first.'

58

There was a young girl of Odessa,
A rather unblushing transgressor;
   When sent to the priest
   The lewd little beast
Began to undress her confessor.

59

There was an old harlot from Dijon
Who in her old age got religion.
  'When I'm dead and gone,'
  Said she, 'I'll take on
The Father, the Son and the Pigeon.'

60

A lissom psychotic named Jane
Once kissed every man on a train.
  Said she, 'Please don't panic,
  I'm just nymphomanic –
It wouldn't be fun, were I sane.'

61

There once was a lady named Mabel
So ready, so willing, so able,
  And so full of spice
  She could name her own price –
Now Mabel's all wrapped up in sable.

62

There've been many illustrious whores –
Salomes, Nell Gwynnes, Pompadours –
  But none so notorious,
  So lovely and glorious
As the mistress of Louis Quatorze.

63

An indolent lass from Iraq
Spent a great deal of time in the sack.
  She could earn a month's pay
  In a night and a day
Without once getting up off her back.

64

A businesslike harlot named Draper
Once tried an unusual caper.
    What made it so nice
    Was you got it half-price
If you brought in her ad from the paper.

65

A hungry old trollop from Yemen
Did a pretty good business with he-men.
    But she gave up all fucking
    In favour of sucking,
For the protein contained in the semen.

66

'Give in to your filthy desires?
I should think not!' cried haughty Miss Myers.
    'The only thing free
    That that part does is pee;
For the other, I've plenty of buyers.'

67

The erotic desires of Miss Myers
Required a great many suppliers.
    When she found, in late years,
    Far too few volunteers,
She brought in a pimp, who got buyers.

68

Said a wicked old madam named Belle,
Whom the preacher was threatening with Hell,
    'I have no regrets,
    No doubts – and no debts,
If I haven't done good, I've done well.'

69

There was a young fellow named Blaine,
And he screwed some disgusting old jane.
   She was ugly and smelly,
   With an awful potbelly,
But . . . well, they were caught in the rain.

70

There was a young lady of Glamis
Who'd undress without any qualms.
   She would strip to the buff
   For enough of the stuff
And freely dispose of her charms.

71

A homely young harlot named Gert
Used to streetwalk until her feet hurt.
   But now she just stands
   Upside-down on her hands
With her face covered up by her skirt.

72

An intelligent whore from Albania
Read books and grew steadily brainier.
   Yet it wasn't her science
   That brought her male clients
But her quite uncontrolled nymphomania.

73

There was a young lady of parts,
Not one of your lower-class tarts;
   She had worked at St John's
   Under ten learned dons
And been certified Mistress of Arts.

74

There was a young lady named Brooke
Who never could learn how to cook.
   But on a divan
   She could please any man –
She knew every damn trick in the book!

75

There was an old girl of Kilkenny
Whose usual charge was a penny.
   For half of that sum
   You might fondle her bum:
A source of amusement to many.

76

A school marm from old Mississippi
Had a quim that was simply zippy.
   The scholars all praised it
   Till finally she raised it
To prices befitting a chippy.

77

Unique is a strumpet of Mazur
In the way that her clientèle pays her:
   A machine that she uses
   Clamps on to her whoosis,
And clocks everybody that lays her.

78

A naked young tart named Roselle
Walked the streets while ringing a bell;
   When asked why she rang it,
   She answered, 'God, dang it!
Can't you see I have something to sell?'

79

The tax-paying whores of the nation
Sent Congress a large delegation
   To convince those old fools
   Their professional tools
Were subject to depreciation.

80

There was a young harlot named Bunny
Whose kisses were sweeter than honey;
   Her callers galore
   Would line up at her door
To take turns in paying her money.

81

That luscious young harlot Miss Birks
(She's the pick of our local sex-works),
   Has serviced the mayor,
   A judge, the surveyor,
And a newsboy (who normally jerks).

82

There was an old whore named McGee
Who was just the right sort for a spree.
   She said, 'For a fuck,
   I charge half a buck,
And throw in the ass-hole for free.'

83

A fearless young spermatozoa
Remarked to an ovum, 'Helloa!
   We'd make a cute foetus,
   But I fear she'd mistreat us –
By the smell of this place, she's a whoah.'

84

A vicious old whore of Albania
Hated men with a terrible mania.
　　With a twitch and a squirm
　　She would hold back your sperm,
And then roll on her face and disdain ya.

85

The tarts in the town of Marseilles
Are brunette from the sun every day.
　　White wine is their piddle,
　　For ten francs they'll diddle –
But their tickets of health, where are they?

86

A tired young trollop of Nome
Was worn out from her toes to her dome.
　　Eight miners came screwing, 　.
　　But she said, 'Nothing doing;
One of you has to go home!'

87

Said a dainty young whore named Miss Meggs,
'The men like to spread my two legs
　　Then slip in between,
　　If you know what I mean,
And leave me the white of their eggs.'

88

There was a young thing from Missouri
Who fancied herself as a houri.
　　Her friends thus forsook her,
　　For a harlot they took her,
And she gave up the role in a fury.

Homoerotica

❦

1

There was a young fellow named Keyte,
Who minced as he walked down the street.
   He wore shoes of bright red
   And playfully said,
'I may not be thtrong, but I'm thweet.'

2

An intense cock addiction is Brent's –
He stands at the stalls in the gents'
   And avidly scans
   Every man's exposed glans
And with such sights his passion contents.

3

An astronomer, pious but odd
(To be honest, a dirty old sod),
   Who'd searched for a sign
   Of the presence divine,
Cried, 'I've just found Uranus, dear God!'

4

An old major, stationed in Nanking,
Was really quite partial to spanking.
   He said, 'S & M
   Is good for the men:
At least, it's much better than wanking.'

5

A glutted debauchee from Frome
Lured beauteous boys to his home,
    Whereupon he would strip them
    A generally whip them
With rods of fine birch or of broom.

6

There was a young pansy named Gene
Who cruised a sadistic Marine.
    Said the man with a smirk
    As they got down to work,
'In this game the Jack beats the Queen.'

7

There was a Scots boy scout from Airdrie
Whose bottom was always kept bared. He
    Explained, 'The scout master
    Can enter me faster,
And a boy scout must aye be prepared. See?'

8

As he lay in his bath, mused Lord Byng,
'O Vimy! What memories you bring:
    That gorgeous young trooper . . .
    Er . . . No! . . . Gladys Cooper!
By Gad, sir! That was a near thing!'

9

While sleeping a sailor from Twickenham
Was aware of a strange object stick in him.
    Before he could turn
    He'd occasion to learn
His shipmate was plunging his prick in him.

10

The grand-niece of Madame DuBarry
Suspected her son was a fairy;
  'It's peculiar,' said she,
  'But he sits down to pee,
And stands when I bathe the canary.'

11

Well buggered was a boy named Depasse
By all of the lads in his class;
  He said, with a yawn:
  'When the novelty's gone,
It's only a pain in the ass.'

12

There was a young fellow, McBride,
Who preferred his trade long, thick and wide.
  But he never rejected
  Whatever erected,
For, 'Peter is peter,' he sighed.

13

A pansy who lived in Khartoum
Took a lesbian up to his room.
  And they argued a lot
  About who should do what,
And how, and with which, and to whom.

14

Said a lesbian lady, 'It's sad;
Of all of the girls that I've had,
  None gave me the thrill
  Of real rapture, until
I learned how to be a tribade.'

15

That naughty old Sappho of Greece
Said, 'What I prefer to a piece,
    Is to have my pudenda
    Rubbed hard by the end o'
The little pink nose of my niece.'

16

The lovers of kooky Miss Fay
Her neighbours believe are all gay,
    For none, when they call,
    Use her front door at all:
They always go in the back way.

17

There was a young sailor named Xavier
Who cared not for God, nor his Saviour.
    He walked on the decks
    Displaying his sex
And was brigged for indecent behaviour.

18

Said Oscar McDingle O'Friggle,
With an almost hysterical giggle,
    'Last night I was sick
    With delight when my prick
Felt dear Alfred's delicious arse wriggle!'

19

There once was a fellow named Bob
Who in sexual ways was a snob.
    One day he went swimmin'
    With twelve naked women
And deserted them all for a gob.

20

A neurotic young playboy named Gleason
Liked boys for no tangible reason.
   A frontal lobotomy
   Cured him of sodomy
But ruined his plans for the season.

21

There was a young fellow of Wadham
Who asked for a ticket to Sodom.
   When they said, 'We prefer
   Not to issue them, sir,'
He said, 'Don't call me "sir"! Call me "modom".'

22

Said the former Prince Edward of Wales:
'I know now what marriage entails,
   So I don't want a girl
   But a jolly young earl,
To solace my passion for males.'

23

There once was a warden of Wadham
Who approved of the folkways of Sodom.
   'For a man might,' he said,
   'Have a very poor head
But be a fine fellow, at bottom.'

24

A whimsical Arab from Aden,
With masculine member well laden,
   Cried, 'Sexual joy
   When shared with a boy
Is better than melon or maiden!'

25

Our ship's captain, nicknamed Old Randy,
Makes advances to any girl handy;
 But when shipwrecked a while
 On a bleak desert isle,
He made do with midshipman Sandy.

26

There was once an effeminate Ottoman.
For the fair sex, I fear, he was not a man.
 He was all up in arms
 Against feminine charms:
'Quite frankly,' he said, 'I'm a bottom man.'

27

There was a young man from Wanamee
Well schooled in the technique of sodomy.
 He buggered with glee
 An old man in a tree,
And remarked with a shrug, 'Won't you pardon me?'

28

There was a captain of MAG 94
More easily had than a two-bit whore.
 He wanted to drink
 And fondle your dink,
But he's not around any more.

29

There was a young man of Oswego,
Whose friends said, 'Be off now, to sea go.'
 He there learned the trick
 Of skinning his prick,
And up arses thrusting his pego.

30

There was an old man of Ramnugger
Who drove a rare trade as a bugger,
  Till a fair young Circassian
  Brought fucking in fashion,
And spoilt all the trade in Ramnugger.

31

A native of Havre de Grâce,
Once tired of cunt said, 'I'll try arse.'
  He unfolded his plan
  To another young man,
Who said, 'Most decidedly, my arse!'

32

There was an old bugger of Como,
Who suddenly cried: 'Ecce Homo!'
  He tracked his man down
  To the heart of the town,
And gobbled him off in the duomo.

33

A convict once, out in Australia,
Said unto his turnkey, 'I'll tail yer.'
  But he said, 'You be buggered,
  You filthy old sluggard,
You're forgetting as I am your gaoler.'

34

A parson who lived near Cremorne
Looked down on all women with scorn.
  E'en a boy's white, fat bum
  Could not make him come,
But an old man's piles gave him the horn.

35

There was a young woman of Norway
Who drove a rare trade in the whore way,
  Till a sodomite viscount
  Brought cunt to a discount,
And the bawdy-house belles to a poor way.

36

There was an old warden of Wadham, he
Was very much given to sodomy,
  But he shyly confessed,
  'I like tongue-fucking best,
God bless my soul, isn't it odd of me?'

37

A youth who seduced a poor lighterman,
Said, 'I'd much sooner fuck than I'd fight a man,
  And although, sir, I find
  You a very good grind,
I must say I've had a much tighter man.'

38

That elegant gigolo, Price,
Remarked, 'Now, it *may* be a vice,
  But one thing I know,
  This dancing for dough
Is something exceedingly nice.'

39

This shortage of help has produced
More kitchen-wise males than it used,
  Like that man of gallantry
  Who, leaving the pantry,
Remarked, 'Well, my cook is well goosed!'

40

If Leo your own birthday marks
You will lust until forty, when starts
   A new pleasure in stamps,
   Boy scouts and their camps,
And fondling nude statues in parks.

41

A serious-minded young slugger
Surprised all when he turned out for rugger;
   Till they found he spent hours
   In the nude in the showers,
Persuading the whole team to bugger.

42

Said an airy young fairy named Jess,
'The oral requires some finesse,
   While in method the anal
   Is terribly banal,
And the trousers will get out of press.'

43

A tourist in Rome, from South Bend,
Decried sodomy to an old friend.
   Leered a visiting Bulgar:
   'You may say it's vulgar,
But you will find it's fun, in the end.'

44

A prince with a temper outrageous
Had a palace replete with young pages.
   They were used for skulduggery
   And much royal buggery,
And he castrated some in his rages.

45

A wonderful tribe are the Sweenies,
Renowned for the length of their peenies.
   The hair on their balls
   Sweeps the floors of their halls,
But they don't look at women, the meanies.

46

A young queer who was much oversexed
Was easily fretted and vexed.
   When out on a date,
   He hardly could wait
To say, 'Turn over, bud; my turn next.'

Alternatives

❦

1

A randy young student named Teddy
With his acolytes used to make ready,
   Till the snoopy old head
   Caught the bugger in bed
Up the arse of his twelve-year-old steady.

2

A pederast living in Arles
Used to bugger the bung of a barrel,
   But was heard to lament,
   'In the old days I went
Up the blue-blooded bum of an earl.'

3

A perverted policeman McClasty
Excels at one sport – pederasty.
   He'll bugger with joy
   Any underage boy
But thinks fornication is nasty.

4

For years a schoolteacher named Field
Reaped the pleasures young boy-asses yield.
   But he's known now as queer
   Since early this year,
When his favourite ass-istant squealed.

5

A spunky young schoolboy named Fred
Used to toss off each night while in bed.
   Said his mother, 'Dear lad,
   That's exceedingly bad:
Jump in here with your mother instead.'

6

There was an old man of Stamboul
With a varicose vein in his tool.
   In attempting to come
   Up a little boy's bum
It burst, and he *did* look a fool.

7

The Sultan of old Istanbul
Had a varicose vein in his tool,
   Which evoked joyous grunts
   From his harem of cunts,
But his boys suffered pain at the stool.

8

A nudist resort in Benares
Took a midget in, all unawares.
   But he made members weep
   For he just couldn't keep
His nose out of private affairs.

9

A remarkable race are the Persians
They have such peculiar diversions.
   They make love all day
   In the regular way,
And save up the night for perversions.

10

It seems that all our perversions
Were known to the Medes and the Persians.
  But the French and the Yanks
  Earn our undying thanks
For inventing some modernised versions.

11

Said a co-ed from Duke University,
When asked about sexual perversity,
  'I find it's OK
  In the old-fashioned way,
But I do like a touch of diversity.'

12

There was a young lover name Marius
Whose approaches to sex were quite various.
  He kept in his files
  All possible styles
That came under the head of nefarious.

13

On the plains of north-central Tibet
They've thought of the strangest thing yet:
  On the ass of a camel
  They pour blue enamel,
And bugger the beast while it's wet.

14

Said the horrible whore of Lahore
While ape-fucking against a door,
  'This orang-utang
  Is better than bhang –
The penis of man's quite a bore.'

15

The eminent Mme DeVue
Was born in a cage at the zoo,
  And the curious rape
  Which made her an ape
Is highly fantastic, if true.

16

A broken-clown harlot named Tupps
Was heard to confess in her cups:
  'The height of my folly
  Was diddling a collie –
But I got a nice price for the pups.'

17

A herder who hailed from Terre Haute
Fell in love with a young nanny-goat.
  The daughter he sired
  Was greatly admired
For her beautiful angora coat.

18

There was a young man from Seattle
Who bested a bull in a battle.
  With fire and unction
  He assumed the bull's function
And deflowered a whole herd of cattle.

19

There was a young man of Wood's Hole
Who had an affair with a mole.
  Though a bit of a nancy
  He did like to fancy
Himself in a dominant role.

20

A yogi from far-off Beirut
For women did not care a hoot.
   But his organ would stand
   In a manner quite grand
When a snake-charmer played on his flute.

21

Two circus girls, richly endowed
With bosoms, won applause long and loud.
   But on tour in Berlin
   They just couldn't win:
The blue-based baboons held the crowd.

22

There was a young fellow named Price
Who dabbled in all sorts of vice:
   He had virgins and boys
   And mechanical toys
And on Mondays he meddled with mice.

23

There was a young person of Jaipur
Who fell madly in love with a viper.
   With screams of delight
   He'd retire each night
With the viper concealed in his diaper.

24

There was an old Scot called McTavish,
Who attempted an anthropoid ravish.
   The object of rape
   Was the wrong sex of ape,
And the anthropoid ravished McTavish.

25

A professor of ethical culture
Once said to his class: ' 'Twould insult your
   Intelligence if
   I said I got stiff
For anything less than a vulture.'

26

A fellow who fucked but as few can
Had a fancy to try with a toucan.
   He owned like a man
   The collapse of his plan:
'I can't – but I bet none of you can!'

27

There was a young woman called Myrtle.
Who once was seduced by a turtle;
   The result of this mate
   Was five crabs and a skate,
Thus proving the turtle was fertile.

28

A deacon, unhappily wed,
Thought to screw a black pig in his bed.
   Now the prick of the pig
   's undeniably big,
And it cork-screwed the deacon instead.

29

A southern hillbilly named Hollis,
Used possums and snakes as his solace;
   His children had scales,
   And prehensile tails,
And voted for Governor Wallace.

30

A round-bottomed babe from Mobile
Longed for years to be screwed by a seal,
   But out at the zoo,
   They just said: 'No can do.'
Though the seal is all hot for the deal.

31

Two she-camels spied on a goat,
And one jealously said: 'You will note
   She leaves the sheik's tent
   With her tail oddly bent,
And hanks of hair pulled out of her coat.'

32

There was a young peasant named Gorse
Who fell madly in love with a horse;
   Said his wife: 'You rapscallion
   The horse is a stallion –
This constitutes grounds for divorce.'

33

A habit obscene and bizarre
Has recently taken papa:
   He brings home young camels
   And other odd mammals
And gives them a go at mama.

34

A scandal involving an oyster
Sent the Countess of Clewes to a cloister.
   She preferred it in bed
   To the Count, so she said,
Being longer and stronger and moister.

35

There was a young girl of Batonger
Used to bring herself off with a conger.
　　When asked how it feels
　　To be pleasured by eels,
She said, 'Just like a man, only longer.'

36

I was thrilled when I went to the zoo:
They allowed me to bugger the gnu!
　　An FRZS
　　Remarked to me, 'Yes,
It's a privilege granted to few.'

37

There was an old man of the Cape,
Who buggered a Barbary ape.
　　Said the ape: 'Sir, your prick
　　Is too long and too thick,
And something is wrong with the shape.'

38

There was an old man of the Cape
Who buggered a Barbary ape.
　　The ape said, 'You fool!
　　You've got a square tool;
You've buggered my arse out of shape.'

39

There was a young man of Bengal,
Who went to a fancy-dress ball.
　　Just for a whim
　　He dressed up as a quim,
And was had by the dog in the hall.

40

There was a musician named Royce,
Who, tired both of women and boys,
    Remarked with a sigh,
    'I fear I must try
Alsatians for my sexual joys.'

41

There was a young fellow named Spiegel
Who had an affair with a seagull.
    What's worse (do you see?),
    It wasn't a she
But he-gull and that is illegal.

42

There was an old person of Sark
Who buggered a pig in the dark.
    The swine, in surprise,
    Murmured, 'God blast your eyes,
Do you take me for Boulton or Park?'

43

There was a young man of St Paul
Whose prick was exceedingly small.
    He could bugger a bug
    At the edge of a rug,
And the bug hardly felt it at all.

44

A nigger in fair St Domingo,
Being blasé and worn, said,
    'By jingo, blast all women and boys,
    I'll try some new joys,'
So he went out and fucked a flamingo.

45

There was an old man of Santander
Who attempted to bugger a gander.
 But that virtuous bird
 Plugged its ass with a turd,
And refused to such low tastes to pander.

46

There was a young man from Toulouse
Who thought he would diddle a goose.
 He hunted and bunted
 To get the thing cunted,
But decided it wasn't no use.

47

There was a young man of Newminster Court
Bugger'd a pig, but his prick was too short.
 Said the hog, 'It's not nice
 But, pray, take my advice:
Make tracks, or by the police you'll be caught.'

48

There was a young man in Peru
Who had nothing whatever to do,
 So he flew to the garret
 And buggered the parrot,
And sent the result to the zoo.

49

A German explorer named Schlichter
Had a yen for a boa constrictor;
 When he lifted the tail,
 Achtung! 'Twas a male.
The constrictor, not Schlichter, was victor.

50

There was a young man from Poughkeepsie
Inclined now and then to get tipsy.
   When afflicted that way
   It was said he would lay
Anything from a sow to a gypsy.

51

There was a young girl who would make
Advances to snake after snake.
   She said, 'I'm not vicious,
   But so superstitious!
I do it for grandmother's sake.'

52

There once was a young man named Cyril
Who was had in a wood by a squirrel,
   And he liked it so good
   That he stayed in the wood
Just as long as the squirrel stayed virile.

53

On the talk show last night Dr Ellis
(The sex shrink) took two hours to tell us,
   'It's all right to enjoy
   A rosy-cheeked boy –
So long as your sheep don't get jealous.'

54

There was an Italian named Bruno
Who said, 'Looking is one thing I do know.
   A woman is fine,
   A man is divine,
But a sheep is *numero uno*.'

55

An Argentine gaucho named Bruno
Once said, 'There is one thing I do know:
   A woman is fine
   And a sheep is divine,
But a llama is *numero uno*!'

56

There was a young lady of Rhodes
Who sinned in unusual modes.
   At the height of her fame
   She abruptly became
The mother of four dozen toads.

57

A keeper in Hamburg's great zoo
Tried to have a young girl kangaroo.
   But she zipped up her pouch,
   And the rascal said, 'Ouch!
You've got a half peter in you.'

58

You've heard of the Duchess of York?
She's twice been blessed by the stork.
   The Duke will fuck
   Naught else but a duck,
While the Duchess she frequents the park.

59

A gruff anthropoid of Piltdown
Had a strange way of going to town:
   With maniacal howls
   He would bugger young owls
And polish his balls on their down.

60

There was a young man from New Haven
Who had an affair with a raven.
   He said with a grin,
   As he wiped of his chin,
'Nevermore! Nevermore!'

61

To Italy went Sinclair Lewis
Documenting the life led by loose
   American drunks,
   But he unpacked his trunks
'Cause Florence slipped him a goose.

62

'At a seance,' said young Johnny Post,
'I was being sucked off by a ghost.
   Someone switched on the lights
   And there in gauze tights,
On his knees, was Tobias, mine host!'

63

Try our Rubber Girlfriend (air-inflatable),
Perennially young (quite insatiable).
   Our satisfied clients,
   From mere midgets to giants,
Say she's incredibly sexy and mateable.

64

A sodomist, fresh out of gaol,
Was desperate for some sort of tail.
   By necessity forced
   He screwed the exhaust
Of a van clearly marked 'Royal Mail'.

65

A young ghost from old Bangladesh
Went out with a girl and got fresh.
　　She said, 'I don't mind
　　High spirits, you'll find,
But I won't have you come in the flesh.'

66

I remarked to the mermaid, 'My dear,
I have pondered on this for a year:
　　As it's fruitless to hunt
　　For a cunt in your front,
May I offer a prick up your ear?

67

A myopic young fellow named Clark
Raped a tall maple tree in the dark.
　　What a splendid surprise!
　　Such tightness and size!
But his foreskin was scraped on the bark.

68

There was a young fellow called Wyatt
Who had a big girl on the quiet.
　　But down on the wharf,
　　He kept a nice dwarf,
Just in case he should go on a diet.

69

When Oedipus entered, erect,
Jocasta screamed, 'Stop! I object.
　　You're a Greek! Screw some other –
　　A goat, or your brother –
Mother-fucking's a little suspect.'

70

Down in Berne, Minister Grew,
There's nothing that fellow won't screw –
　　From queens down to cooks
　　They're all on his books,
And he dabbles in sodomy too.

71

There once was a kiddie named Carr
Caught a man on top of his ma.
　　As he saw him stick 'er,
　　He said, with a snicker,
You do it much faster than pa.'

72

It's alleged that the Emperor Titius
Had a penchant for pleasantries vicious.
　　He took two of his nieces
　　And fucked them to pieces,
And said it was simply delicious.

73

There was a young fellow named Blades
Whose favourite fruit was young maids;
　　Though sheep, nigger boys, whores,
　　And the knot-holes in doors
Were by no means exempt from his raids.

74

There was a young party of Bicester
Who wanted to bugger his sister,
　　But not liking dirt
　　He purchased a squirt
and rinsed out the part with a clyster.

75

A forward young fellow named Tarr
Had a habit of goosing his ma;
   'Go pester your sister,'
   She said, when he kissed her,
'I've trouble enough with your pa.'

76

There was an old man from Fort Drum
Whose son was incredibly dumb;
   When he urged him ahead
   He went down instead,
For he thought to succeed meant succumb.

77

There was a young farmer of Nantes
Whose conduct was gay and gallant,
   For he fucked all his dozens
   Of nieces and cousins,
In addition, of course, to his aunt.

78

There was an incestuous Corsican
Whose only delight was to force kin.
   He fucked his kid sister
   Till he raised such a blister
That now he can't pull back his foreskin.

79

There was a young man from Liberia
Who was forced to flee to the interior.
   He'd buggered a brother,
   His father and mother –
He considered his sisters inferior.

Married Lives

❧

1

I did feel obliged to friend Fife
For the overnight use of his wife.
　　But he dropped in today
　　And insisted on pay –
Such sordidness sours me on life.

2

There once was a *maître d'hôtel*,
Who said, 'They can all go to hell!
　　They make love to my wife
　　And it ruins my life,
For the worst is, they do it so well!'

3

There was a young lady of Condover
Whose husband had ceased to be fond of her.
　　He could not forget
　　He had wooed a brunette
But peroxide had now made a blonde of her.

4

There was a young lady of Eton
Whose figure had plenty of meat on.
　　She said, 'Marry me, dear,
　　And you'll find that my rear
Is a nice place to warn your cold feet on.'

5

The Reverend Mr Golightly
Was cuckolded daily and nightly.
    He murmured, 'Oh dear:
    I'd fain interfere –
If I knew how to do so politely.'

6

A near-sighted fellow named Walter,
Led a glamorised lass to the altar;
    A beauty he thought her,
    Till some soap and water
Made her look like the Rock of Gibraltar.

7

There was a young fellow named Hammer
Who had an unfortunate stammer.
    'The b–bane of my life,'
    He said, 'is m–my wife.
D–d–d–d–d–d–damn her.'

8

A progressive and young Eskimo
Grew tired of his squaw, and so
    Slipped out of his hut
    To look for a slut
Who knew the very fine art of blow.

9

A young trapeze artist named Bract
Is faced by a very sad fact:
    Imagine his pain,
    When, again and again,
He catches his wife in the act!

10

There was a young fellow named Keating
Whose pride took a terrible beating.
   That happens to males
   When they learn the details
Of their wives' extra-marital cheating.

11

An eager young bride, Mrs Strong,
Thought that passion would last all night long;
   And her husband's capacity
   Would match her voracity –
But (alas!) it transpired she was wrong.

12

An astonished young bride in Hong Kong
Found her husband abnormally strong.
   She knew about sex
   And its heady effects,
But thought thirty-two times might be wrong.

13

There was an old fellow of Lyme
Who lived with three wives at a time.
   When asked, 'Why the third?'
   He replied, 'One's absurd;
And bigamy, sir, is a crime.'

14

There was a young lady of Pinner
Whose hubby came home to his dinner;
   And guess what he saw
   As he opened the door?
The butt of the man who was in her.

15

Sighed a newlywed damsel of Wheeling,
'A honeymoon sounds so appealing,
   But for nearly two weeks
   I've heard only bed squeaks
And seen nothing but cracks in the ceiling.'

16

The bedsprings next door jounce and creak:
They have kept me awake for a week.
   Why do newlyweds
   Select squeaky beds
To perfect their fucking technique?

17

To his bride said a numskull named Clarence,
'I trust you will show some forbearance.
   My sexual habits
   I picked up from rabbits,
And occasionally watching my parents.'

18

Have you heard of the widow O'Reilly
Who esteemed her late husband so highly
   That, in spite of the scandal,
   Her umbrella handle
Was made of his *membrum virile*?

19

A widow who lived in Rangoon
Hung a black-ribboned wreath o'er her womb,
   'To remind me,' she said,
   'Of my husband, who's dead;
And of what put him into his tomb.'

20

The toe of a postman from Dallas
Developed a sizeable callous.
　　His wife wistfully said
　　How she wished that, instead,
It had been on the head of his phallus.

21

There was a young man with a prick
Which into his wife he would stick
　　Every morning and night
　　If it stood up all right –
Not a very remarkable trick.

His wife had a nice little cunt:
It was hairy, and soft, and in front,
　　And with this she would fuck him,
　　Though sometimes she'd suck him –
A charming, if commonplace, stunt.

22

There was a young fellow from Wark
Who, when he screws, has to bark.
　　His wife is a bitch
　　With a terrible itch,
So the town never sleeps after dark.

23

A newlywed man of Peru
Found himself in a terrible stew:
　　His wife was in bed
　　Much deader than dead
And so he had no one to screw.

24

There was a young fellow named Kelly
Who preferred his wife's ass to her belly.
　He shrieked with delight
　As he ploughed through the shite,
And filled up her hole with his jelly.

25

There was a young fellow named Fyfe
Whose marriage was ruined for life,
　For he had an aversion
　To every perversion,
And only liked fucking his wife.

Well, one year the poor woman struck,
And she wept, and she cursed at her luck,
　And said, 'Where have you gotten us
　With your goddamn monotonous
Fuck after fuck after fuck?'

26

There was a young man named McNamiter
With a tool of prodigious diameter,
　But it wasn't the size
　Gave the girls a surprise,
But his rhythm – iambic pentameter.

27

'I once knew a harlot named Lou –
And a versatile girl she was, too.
　After ten years of whoredom
　She perished of boredom
When she married a jackass like you!'

28

An octogenarian Jew
To his wife remained steadfastly true.
   This was not from compunction,
   But due to dysfunction
Of his spermatic glands – nuts to you.

29

There was a gay Countess of Dufferin,
One night while her husband was covering,
   Just to chaff him a bit
   She said, 'You old shit,
I can buy a dildo for a sovereign.'

30

At his wedding a bridegroom named Crusoe
Was embarrassed to find his prick grew so.
   His eager young bride
   Pulled him quickly astride
And was screwed while still wearing her trousseau.

31

There was an old couple in Sayville
Whose habits were quite medieval:
   They would strip to the skin
   Then each take a pin
And pick lint from the other one's navel.

32

A hot-tempered girl of Caracas
Was wed to a samba-mad jackass;
   When he started to cheat her
   With a dark senorita
She kicked him right in the maracas.

33

I wonder what my wife will want tonight;
Wonder if the wife will fuss and fight?
 I wonder can she tell
 That I've been raising hell;
Wonder if she'll know that I've been tight?

My wife is just as nice as nice can be,
I hope she doesn't feel too nice toward me,
 For an afternoon of joy
 Is hell on the old boy.
I wonder what the wife will want tonight!

34

There was a young man named Moritz
Who was subject to passionate fits,
 But his pleasure in life
 Was to suck off his wife
As he swung by his knees from her tits.

35

There was a young parson of Harwich,
Tried to grind his betrothed in a carriage.
 She said, 'No, you young goose,
 Just try self-abuse,
And the other we'll try after marriage.'

36

FOR WIDOWER – wanted – housekeeper,
Not too bloody refined, a light sleeper;
 When employer's inclined,
 Must be game for a grind,
Pay generous, mind, but can't keep her.

37

A king sadly said to his queen,
'In parts you have grown far from lean.'
  'I don't give a damn,
  You've always liked ham,'
She replied, and he gasped, 'How obscene!'

38

A shiftless young fellow of Kent,
Had his wife fuck the landlord for rent;
  But as she grew older,
  The landlord grew colder,
And now they live out in a tent.

39

There was an old person of Goshem
Who took out his bollocks to wash 'em.
  His wife said, 'Now, Jack,
  If you don't put them back,
I'll step on the buggers and squash 'em.'

40

There was a young man of Ostend
Whose wife caught him fucking her friend.
  'It's no use, my duck,
  Interrupting our fuck,
For I'm damned if I draw till I spend.'

41

I think I must speak to my wife:
She's been giving free tail to old Fife.
  It isn't the screwing
  I mind the bitch doing,
It's the 'free' part that's causing the strife!

42

A suspicious old husband from Funtua
To his wife said, 'How bulky in front you are.
   You have not been imprudent,
   I hope, with some student?'
She replied, 'Really, dear, how blunt you are!'

43

To his bride said the lynx-eyed detective,
'Can it be that my eyesight's defective?
   Has your west tit the least bit
   The best of the east tit?
Or is it a trick of perspective?'

44

A newlywed husband named Lyneham
Asked his bride if she'd first 'sixty-nine' him.
   When she just shook her head,
   He sighed and then said,
'Well, if we can't lick 'em, let's jine 'em.'

45

Of my husband I do not ask much,
Just an all mod. and con. little hutch;
   Bank account in my name,
   With cheque book to same,
Plus a small fee for fucking and such.

46

There was an old man of Dundee
Who came home as drunk as can be;
   He wound up the clock
   With the end of his cock,
And buggered his wife with the key.

47

There was an old fellow of Fife,
Who lived a lascivious life;
   When his organ was limp
   Like an over-boned shrimp,
He brought what was left to his wife.

48

When the judge with his wife having sport,
Proved suddenly two inches short,
   The good lady declined,
   And the judge had her fined
By proving contempt of his court.

49

A mortician who practised in Fife
Made love to the corpse of his wife.
   'How could I know, judge?
   She was cold and did not budge –
Just the same as she'd been all her life.'

50

A remarkable fellow named Clarence
Had learned self-control from his parents.
   With his wife in the nude
   He'd just sit there and brood,
And practise the art of forbearance.

51

There once was a matron of Ottawa
Whose husband, she said, thought a lot of her;
   Which, to give him his due
   Was probably true,
Since he'd sired twenty kids, all begot of her.

52

In summer he said she was fair,
In autumn her charms were still there:
  But he said to his wife,
  In the winter of life,
'There's no spring in your old *derrière*.'

53

A husband who lived in Tiberias,
Once laughed himself almost delirious.
  But he laughed at his wife,
  And she took a sharp knife,
With results that were quite deleterious.

54

There was an old man of Calcutta
Who spied through a chink in the shutter;
  But all he could spot
  Was his wife's throbbing twat
And the arse of the bloke that was up her.

55

'Adultery,' said Joseph, 'is nice;
If once is all right – better twice.
  This doubling of rations
  Improves my sensations,
For the plural of "spouse", friend, is "spice".'

56

A newlywed couple from Goshen
Spent their honeymoon sailing the ocean.
  In twenty-eight days
  They got laid eighty ways:
Imagine such fucking devotion!

57

A pretty wife living in Tours
Demanded her daily amour.
  But the husband said, 'No!
  It's too much. Let it go!
My backsides are dragging the floor.'

58

There was a young housewife of Ayr,
Whose husband's homecomings were rare.
  Had he danced on her chest
  She'd have felt quite at rest,
For at least she'd have known he was there.

59

A lady was once heard to weep,
'My figure no more I can keep.
  It's my husband's demand
  For a tit in each hand,
But the bastard will walk in his sleep!'

Pleasing Yourself

❦

1

To her grandson said nosy Miz' Todd,
'Do you spend your nights rubbing your rod?
   Your old man, as a kid
   Most certainly did;
If you don't do it too, you're quite odd.'

2

Beneath the spreading chestnut tree
The village smith, he stands,
   Amusing himself
   By abusing himself
With his toilworn horny hands.

3

A nice little schoolboy named Ted
Fell asleep on the family bed.
   O, what could be sweeter?
   One hand on his Peter
Pan book and one under his head.

4

'You know,' said the King of the Czechs,
'I too have a problem in sex.
   The men of my nation
   Prefer masturbation;
My women are physical wrecks.'

5

There was a young fellow named Chisholm
Afflicted with skin erotism.
    In bathing, he'd rub
    His prick in the tub
Till the water was soapy with jism.

6

There was a young man from Darjeeling
Whose dong reached up to the ceiling.
    In the electric-light socket
    He'd put it and rock it –
Oh God! What a wonderful feeling!

7

There was an asexual bigot
Whose cock only served as a spigot,
    Till a jolly young whore
    Taught him tricks by the score,
Now his greatest delight is to frig it.

8

A milkmaid there was, with a stutter,
Who was lonely and wanted a futter.
    She had nowhere to turn,
    So she diddled a churn,
And managed to come with the butter.

9

When a man's too old even to toss off, he
Can sometimes be consoled by philosophy.
    One frequently shows a
    Strong taste for Spinoza
When one's balls are beginning to ossify.

10

The new cinematic emporium
Is not just a super-sensorium,
   But a highly effectual
   Heterosexual
Mutual masturbatorium.

11

There was once a young man from Venice
Who played a good game of lawn tennis;
   But the game he liked best,
   Far more than the rest,
He played with two balls and one penis.

12

There was a cute quirp from Calcutta
Who was fond of churning love-butta.
   One night she was heard mutta
   That her quim was a-flutta
For the thing she called 'Utterly-Utta!'

13

Another young lady named Hicks
Spent all her time thinking of pricks,
   And it was her odd whim
   To tickle her quim
Till it foamed like a bottle of Dicks.

14

There was a young fellow from Lees
Who handled his tool with great ease.
   This continual friction
   Made his sex a mere fiction,
But the callus hangs down to his knees.

15

There was a young fellow from Dallas
Who enjoyed doing things with his phallus.
    So many tricks did he try
    It became, by and by,
Little more than a leather-tough callus.

16

A geneticist living in Delft
Scientifically played with himself,
    And when he was done,
    He labelled it: SON,
And filed it away on a shelf.

17

Poor old Robinson Crusoe!
He had no woman to screw, so
    He'd sit on a rock
    And play with his cock
(Or he'd get his man Friday to do so).

18

There once was a sailor named Gasted
A swell guy, as long as he lasted.
    He could jerk himself off
    In a basket, aloft,
Or a breeches-buoy swung from the masthead.

19

There was a young lady named Mandel
Who caused quite a neighbourhood scandal
    By coming out bare
    On the main village square
And frigging herself with a candle.

20

There was a young lady named May
   Who frigged herself in the hay.
     She bought a pickle –
     One for a nickel –
And wore all the warts away!

21

There was an Old Man of the Mountain
Who frigged himself into a fountain.
     Fifteen times had he spent,
     Still he wasn't content,
He simply got tired of the counting.

22

There was a young fellow from Yale
Whose face was exceedingly pale.
     He spent his vacation
     In self-masturbation
Because of the high price of tail.

23

There was a young man of high station
Attached to the Chinese Legation.
     He liked to be fucked,
     And adored being sucked,
But he revelled in pure masturbation.

24

There was a young man of St Paul's
Possessed the most useless of balls.
     Till at last, at the Strand,
     He managed a stand,
And tossed himself off in the stalls.

25

An innocent boy in Lapland
Was told that frigging was grand.
  But at his first trial
  He said with a smile,
'I've had the same feeling by hand.'

26

There was an old Chinaman drunk
Who went for a sail in his junk.
  He was dreaming of Venus
  And tickling his penis,
Till he floated away in the spunk.

27

There was a young woman of Croft
Who played with herself in a loft,
  Having reasoned that candles
  Could never cause scandals,
Besides which they did not go soft.

28

A fellow who lived in Sidcup
Had such trouble getting it up,
  He lay on his bed
  And wanked off instead.
That's life, as it's lived in Sidcup!

29

There was an Archbishop of Rheims
Who played with himself in his dreams.
  On his nightshirt in front
  He painted a cunt,
Which made his spend gush forth in streams.

30

There was a young man from Montrose
Who could diddle himself with his toes.
   He did it so neat
   He fell in love with his feet,
And christened them Myrtle and Rose.

31

Oh, that supple young man of Montrose
Who tickled his tail with his toes!
   His landlady said,
   As she made up his bed,
'My God! How that man blows his nose!'

32

There was a young man named M'Gurk
Who dosed off one night after work,
   He had a wet dream
   But awoke with a scream
Just in time to give it a jerk.

33

A squeamish young fellow named Brand
Thought caressing his penis was grand,
   But he viewed with distaste
   The gelatinous paste
That it left in the palm of his hand.

34

There was a young man of Calcutta
Who jerked himself off in the gutter.
   But the tropical sun
   Played hell with his gun
And turned all his cream into butter.

35

There was a young fellow named Bream.
Who never had dreamt a wet dream,
   For when lacking a whore
   He'd just bore out the core
Of an apple, and fuck it through cream.

36

There was a young naval cadet
Whose dreams were unusually wet
   When he dreamt of his wedding
   He soaked up the bedding
And the wedding ain't taken place yet.

37

A lecherous Northumbrian druid,
Whose mind was filthy and lewd,
   Awoke from a trance
   With his hand in his pants
On a lump of pre-seminal fluid.

38

There was a young girl of Cohoes
Who jerked herself off with her nose.
   She said, 'Yes, I done it,
   But just for the fun it
Afforded the folk of Cohoes.'

39

A young jacker-off of Cawnpore
Never felt a desire for more.
   In bold self-reliance
   He cried out his defiance
Of the joys of the fairy and whore.

40

Said another young woman of Croft,
Amusing herself in the loft,
  'A salami or wurst
  Is what I should choose first –
With bologna you know you've been boffed.'

41

There was a young man from Aberdeen
Who invented a jerking machine.
  On the twenty-fifth stroke
  The goddamn thing broke
And beat his balls to a cream.

42

There was a young fellow named Veach
Who fell fast asleep on the beach.
  His dreams of nude women
  Had his proud organ brimming
And squirting on all within reach.

43

A soldier named Dougall McDougall
Was caught jacking off in his bugle.
  Said they of the army,
  'We think that you're barmy,'
Said he, 'It's the new way to frugle.'

44

There was a pianist named Liszt
Who played with one hand while he pissed,
  But as he grew older
  His technique grew bolder,
And in concert jacked off with his fist.

45

There was a young fellow named Rule
Who went to a library school.
  As he fingered the index
  His thoughts ran to sex,
And his blood all ran to his tool.

46

There was a young fellow named Rummy
Who delighted in whipping his dummy.
  He played pocket pool
  With his happy old tool
Till his shorts and his pants were all comey.

47

A thrifty old man named McEwen
Enquired, 'Why be bothered with screwing?
  It's safer and cleaner
  To finger your wiener,
And besides you can see what you're doing.'

48

There was a young girl named Miss Randall
Who thought it beneath her to handle
  A young fellow's pole,
  So, instead, her hot hole
She contented by means of a candle.

49

A professor who hailed from Podunk
And was rather too frequently drunk,
  Said, 'Sometimes I think
  That I can parse pink:
Let me see – it is pink, pank and punk.'

50

Let us now broach a firkin to Durkin,
Addicted to jerkin' his gherkin;
  His wife said, 'Now, Durkin,
  By jerkin' your gherkin
You're shirkin' your firkin' – you bastard.'

51

There once was a hardened old bitch
With a motorised self-frigger which
  She would use with delight,
  Far into the night –
Twenty bucks – Abercrombie & Fitch.

52

There was a young man of Calcutta
  Who thought he would do a smart trick,
So anointed his arsehole with butter,
  And in it inserted his prick.
    It was not for greed after gold,
  It was not for thirst after pelf;
    'Twas simply because he'd been told
  To bloody well bugger himself.

53

There was a young man who thought, 'Why
Can't I bugger myself, if I'm spry?
  If I put my mind to it,
  I'm sure I can do it –
You never can tell, till you try!'

54

There was a young fellow of Mayence
Who fucked his own arse in defiance
  Not only of custom
  And morals, dad-bust him,
But most of the known laws of science.

55

There was a young man of Arras
Who laid himself out on the grass,
   And with no little trouble
   He bent himself double
And stuck his prick well up his arse.

56

There was a young man from Madrid
Who discovered when only a kid
   That by lying supine
   And twisting his spine,
He could suck his own cock – so he did.

57

There was a young man named Pete
Who was a bit indiscreet.
   He pulled on his dong
   Till it grew very long
And actually dragged in the street.

58

She made a thing of soft leather,
And topped off the end with a feather.
   When she poked it inside her
   She took off like a glider,
And gave up her lover forever.

59

When a girl, young Elizabeth Barrett,
Was found by her ma in a garret,
   She had shoved up a diamond
   As far as her hymen,
And was ramming it home with a carrot.

60

Don't dip your wick in a Wac,
Don ride the breast of a Wave,
   Just sit in the sand
   And do it by hand,
And buy bonds with the money you save.

61

Under the spreading chestnut tree
The village smithy sat,
   Amusing himself
   By abusing himself
And catching the load in his hat.

62

A charming young lady named Randall
Has a clap that the doctors can't handle.
   So this lovely, lorn floozie,
   With her poor, damaged coosie,
Must take her delight with a candle.

Shapes and Sizes

❦

1

There was a young girl from Taipei
Who was voted the Queen of the May;
    But the pole she went round
    Wasn't stuck in the ground
But attached to a young man named Wei.

2

Said a Guardsman, observing his charger:
'I do wish my tassel were larger.
    Could I change with my horse,
    I should do so, of course –
And put in for high stud-fees, like Rajah.'

3

A young British army deserter
Asked his girlfriend if intercourse hurt her.
    She replied, 'Sometimes, Tommy,
    If it's big, like salami,
But not when it's like your frankfurter.'

4

Said an ardent young man with a grin,
'I think it is time to begin.'
    Said the girl, with a sneer,
    'With what? Why your pee-er
Is scarcely as long as a pin!'

5

There was a young fellow of Perth
Whose balls were the finest on earth.
   They grew to such size
   That one won a prize
And goodness knows what they were worth.

6

A young man whose sight was myopic
Thought sex an incredible topic.
   So poor were his eyes
   That despite its great size
His penis appeared microscopic.

7

There was a young man named Zerubbabel
Who had only one real and one rubber ball.
   When asked if his pleasure
   Was only half-measure,
He replied, 'That is highly improbable.'

8

The one-balled new spouse of our Kitty
We feel is deserving of pity,
   Except that the catch is
   His one-balledness matches
Our Kitty, who has but one titty.

9

Another young fellow named Hatch,
His wife had a cubical snatch.
   He – in no way outwitted
   (She was also three-titted) –
Extracted a square root to match.

10

There once was a Duchess of Bruges
Whose cunt was incredibly huge.
  Said the king to this dame
  As he thunderously came:
'*Mon Dieu! Après moi, le déluge!*'

11

There was a young man from Natal
And Sue was the name of his gal.
  He went out one day
  For a rather long way –
In fact, right up Sue'z Canal.

12

There was a young lady of Nantes
Whose figure was *très élégante*.
  But her cunt was so small
  It was no good at all
Except for *la plume de ma tante*.

13

There was a young lady of Harrow
Who complained that her cunt was too narrow,
  For times without number
  She would use a cucumber,
But could not encompass a marrow.

14

There was a young girl in Berlin
Who was fucked by an elderly Finn.
  Though he diddled his best,
  And fucked her with zest,
She kept asking, 'Hey, pop, is it in?'

15

'Active balls?' said an old man of Stoneham.
'I regret that I no longer own 'em.
   But I hasten to say
   They were good in their day –
De mortuis nil nisi bonum.'

16

An organist playing at York
Had a prick that could hold a small fork,
   And between obligatos
   He'd munch at tomatoes,
And keep up his strength while at work.

17

I got this from the fellow what owns it:
He declared that he boasted one mo' nut
   Than most people sport,
   But was terribly short
In the part you might stick through a doughnut.

18

There was a young girl from Hong Kong
Who said, 'You are utterly wrong
   To say my vagina
   's the largest in China,
Just because of your mean little dong.'

19

There once was a sensitive bride
Who ran when the groom she espied.
   When she looked at his swiver
   They had to revive her,
But when he got it well in, she just sighed.

20

A mathematician named Hall
Has a hexahedronical ball,
   And the cube of its weight
   Times his pecker, plus eight,
Is his phone number – give him a call.

21

There was a young fellow named Hall
Who confessed, 'I have only one ball,
   But the size of my prick
   Is God's dirtiest trick
For the girls always ask, 'Is that all?'

22

There was a young fellow named Prynne
Whose prick was so short and so thin,
   His wife found she needed
   A microscope (she did)
To tell if he'd gotten it in.

23

There was a young man from Berlin
Whose prick was the size of a pin.
   Said his girl, with a laugh,
   As she fondled his shaft,
'Well, this won't be much of a sin.'

24

There was a young fellow of Warwick
Who had reason for feeling euphoric,
   For he could, by election,
   Have triune erection –
Ionic, Corinthian, Doric.

25

There was a young Marquis of Landsdowne,
Who tried hard to keep his great stands down.
   Said he, 'But that I thought
   I should break it off short,
My penis I'd hold with both hands down.'

26

An astonished young lady named Bissell
Let out a lascivious whistle
   When her boyfriend stripped nude.
   He remarked, 'Though it's crude,
Please observe that it's muscle, not missile!'

27

A sailor who slept in the sun
Woke to find his fly-buttons undone.
   He remarked with a smile,
   'By Jove, a sundial –
And now it's a quarter past one!'

28

In the Garden of Eden lay Adam
Complacently stroking his madam,
   And great was his mirth,
   For he knew that on earth
There were only two balls – and he had 'em.

29

There was a young fellow of Greenwich
Whose balls were all covered with spinach.
   He had such a tool
   It was wound on a spool,
And he reeled it out inich by inich.

But this tale has an unhappy finich,
For, due to the sand in the spinach,
   His bollocks grew rough
   And wrecked his wife's muff,
And scratched up her thatch in the scrimmage.

30

A fellow whose surname was Hunt
Trained his cock to perform a slick stunt:
   This versatile spout
   Could be turned inside out,
Like a glove, and be used as a cunt.

31

There was a young bride of Antigua
Whose husband said, 'Dear me, how big you are!'
   Said the girl, 'What damn'd rot!
   Why, you've often felt my twot,
My legs and my arse and my figua!'

32

A biblical party called Ham
Cried, 'Cuss it, I don't give a damn!
   My father's yard measure
   I view with great pleasure,
Such a bloody great battering ram!'

33

There was a young man of Lahore
Whose prick was one inch and no more.
  It was all right for keyholes
  And little girls' pee-holes,
But not worth a damn with a whore.

34

There once was a lady from Kansas
Whose cunt was as big as Bonanzas.
  It was nine inches deep
  And the sides were quite steep –
It had whiskers like General Carranza's.

35

There was a young fellow from Florida
Who liked a friend's wife, so he borrowed her.
  When they got into bed
  He cried, 'God strike me dead!
This ain't a cunt – it's a corridor!'

36

There was an old man of Connaught
Whose prick was remarkably short.
  When he got into bed
  The old woman said,
'This isn't a prick, it's a wart.'

37

There was a young fellow named Carse
Whose bollocks were fashioned from brass.
  When they tinkled together
  They played *Stormy Weather*
And lightning shot out of his arse.

38

Pubic hair is put there for a reason
That is evident in the cold season:
   For the balls it's a muff,
   For the rod it's a ruff;
And it keeps the vagina from freezin'.

39

There was a young lady from Spain
Whose face was exceedingly plain,
   But her cunt had a pucker
   That made the men fuck her,
Again, and again, and again.

40

There was a young lady of Lincoln
Who said that her cunt was a pink 'un,
   So she had a prick lent her
   Which turned it magenta,
This artful young lady of Lincoln.

41

There was once a newspaper vendor,
A person of dubious gender,
   He'd agree, if you'd queue,
   To allow you to view
His remarkable double pudenda.

42

There was a young man of Toulouse
Who had a deficient prepuce.
   But the foreskin he lacked
   He made up in his sac,
The result was: his balls were too loose.

43

There never was anything neater
Than the Bishop of Rochester's peter.
  In the heat of a clinch
  It would swell from an inch
To just a bit short of a metre.

44

There was an old man of Brienz,
The length of whose cock was immense.
  With one swerve he could plug
  A boy's bottom in Zug
And a kitchen-maid's cunt in Coblenz.

45

The tool of the Bishop of Truro
Was a rich colorado maduro,
  Said a real *cognoscenta*,
  'His balls were magenta,
Shot through with chiaroscuro.'

46

Take the case of a lady named Frost
Whose organ is three feet across.
  It's the best part of valour
  To bugger the gal, or
One's apt to fall in and get lost.

47

There's a charming young girl in Tobruk
Who refers to her quim as a nook.
  It's deep and it's wide –
  You can curl up inside
In a nice easy chair, with a book.

48

Hermaphrodites cause a sensation
By their odd, two-in-one combination.
　Concave and convex,
　They are partly each sex,
And a dilly at self-fornication!

49

When I was a baby, my penis
Was as white as the buttocks of Venus.
　But now, 'tis as red
　As her nipples, instead –
All because of the feminine genus!

50

There was a seductive Brazilian
Who dyed her pudenda vermilion.
　Admiring her work,
　She said with a smirk:
'That's certainly one in a million!'

51

Said a girl, as she walked down the Strand,
To her friend who was too plainly manned:
　'Dear, it's catching the eye
　Of each girl we pass by.
Can't you cover it up with your hand?'

52

An explorer returned from Australia
Reported lost paraphernalia:
　A Zeiss microscope,
　And his personal hope,
Which had vanished with his genitalia.

53

There was a gay parson of Norton
Whose prick, although thick, was a short 'un.
    To make up for this loss
    He had balls like a horse,
And never spent less than a quartern.

54

There was a young maiden from Ossett
Whose quim was nine inches across it.
    Said a young man named Tong,
    With tool nine inches long,
'I'll put t' bugger in, if I loss it.'

55

There was a young fellow of Merton
Who went out with only his shirt on,
    From which did peep shyly
    His *membrum virile*,
For people to animadvert on.

56

There was a young lawyer named Rex
Who was sadly deficient in sex.
    Arraigned for exposure
    He said, with composure,
'*De minimis non curat lex.*'

57

In the speech of his time did the Bard
Refer to his prick as his 'yard';
    But sigh no more, madams,
    'Twas no longer than Adam's
Or mine – and not one half so hard!

58

The prick of a young man of Kew
Showed veins that were azure of hue.
  Its head was quite red
  So he waved it, and said,
'Three cheers for the red, white and blue.'

59

There was a young man of Coblenz
Whose equipment was simply immense.
  It took forty-four draymen,
  A priest and three laymen
To carry it thither and thence.

60

Queen Mary found Scotsmen are built
With a truly remarkable tilt:
  To her royal surprise
  Every member would rise
Each time she reached under a kilt.

61

Dame Catherine of Ashton-on-Lynches
Got on with her grooms and her wenches:
  She went down on the gents,
  And probed the girls' vents
With a clitoris reaching six inches.

62

There was once a haughty old baronet
With a prick twice as long as a clarinet.
  If the thing ever dangled
  'Twould be stepped on and mangled
So he kept it tucked inside a hair-i-net.

63

There was a young fellow named Nick
Who was terribly proud of his prick.
   Without fear it might bend
   He would bounce on its end,
As he said, 'It's my own pogostick.'

64

Said the aged Chief Rabbi of Joppa,
'I think circumcision's improper
   If the organ is small;
   But I don't mind at all
About taking a slice off a whopper.'

65

For his concert a flautist named Kress
Was in such a hurry to dress
   That, on a high run,
   His fly came undone –
His organ got raves from the press.

66

There was a young man of Devizes,
Whose balls were of different sizes.
   His tool, when at ease,
   Reached down to his knees;
Oh, what must it be when it rises?

67

There was a young man of Devizes
Whose balls were of different sizes.
   One was so small
   It was no ball at all
But the other was large, and won prizes.

68

No wonder that man of Devizes
Is the winner of so many prizes:
   His rod, when at ease,
   Goes twice round his knees
And tickles his chin when it rises.

69

A mechanical marvel was Bill.
He'd a tool that was shaped like a quill;
   With this fabulous dink
   He could squirt purple ink
And decorate lampshades at will.

70

There was a Greek sailor from Thalia
Who knew several ways to regale ya.
   His principal trump
   Was his cute little rump
Supporting his huge genitalia.

71

There was a young Turkish cadet –
And this is the damnedest one yet –
   His tool was so long
   And incredibly strong
He could bugger six Greeks *en brochette*.

72

There was a young man of Nantucket
Whose prick was so long he could suck it:
   He said with a grin
   As he wiped off his chin,
'If my ear were a cunt I could fuck it.'

73

A daring young doctor named Edison
Decided old standards to jettison.
   He measured men's tools
   By linguistical rules,
And established new canons of medicine.

74

A well-equipped fellow in school
Has the whole class admiring his tool.
   This magnificent dong
   Is quite twelve inches long,
Though it isn't much use as a rule.

75

There was a young lady of Chester
Who fell in love with a jester.
   Though her breath came out hotly
   At the sight of his motley,
It was really his wand that impressed her.

76

When he tried to insert his huge whanger
A young man aroused his girl's anger.
   As they strove in the dark,
   She was heard to remark:
'What you need is a Zeppelin hangar.'

77

There once was a handsome young sheik
With a marvellous penile physique.
   Its length and its weight
   Made it look really great,
But he fell very short on technique.

78

Lady Reginald Humphries (belie-
Ve it or not) had a vulva so wee
   She disposed of the sexual
   Needs of Lord Rex through a l-
Audably disciplined flea.

79

Said a snooty young thing from Australia:
'Now concerning the male genitalia,
   Men brag of their size
   Till you're sure you've a prize,
Then exhibit wee paraphernalia.'

80

There was a young fellow called Chubb
Who joined a smart buggery club;
   But his parts were so small,
   He was no use at all,
And they promptly refunded his sub.

81

A lady of features cherubic
Was famed for her area pubic;
   When they asked its size,
   She said with surprise:
'Are you speaking of square feet, or cubic?'

82

There once was a judge of Assize
Whose bollocks were not the same size.
   He'd look at the right
   With a gasp of delight,
But the left one brought tears to his eyes.

83

There was a young man of Ghent,
Whose tool was so long, that it bent;
   To save himself trouble,
   He put it in double,
And instead of coming, he went.

84

There was a young man from Hong Kong
Who had a trifurcated prong:
   A small one for sucking,
   A large one for fucking,
And a *honey* for beating a gong.

85

There was a young maiden named Hoople
Whose bosom was triple, not douple;
   So she had one removed
   But it grew back improved
And at present her front is quadruple.

86

There once was a young man named Lanny
The size of whose prick was uncanny.
   His wife, the poor dear,
   Took it into her ear
And it came out the hole in her fanny.

87

Another young fellow named Kimble
Had a prick most exceedingly nimble,
   But so fragile and tender
   And dainty and slender
He kept it encased in a thimble.

88

When the Bishop of Solomon's diocese
Was stricken with elephantiasis,
　　The public beheld
　　His balls as they swelled
By paying exorbitant priocese.

89

There was a young woman named Sally
Who loved an occasional dally.
　　She sat on the lap
　　Of a well-endowed chap
And said, 'Oo, you're right up my alley!'

90

A lady who came from Mobile
Had a cunt made of Bessemer steel.
　　She could only get thrills
　　From mechanical drills
Or an off-centre emery wheel.

91

Come and see our French goods – you can try 'em,
Fit them on for right size when you buy 'em:
　　Strong, smooth and reversible,
　　The thinnest dispersible;
Any *odd* shape you need, we supply 'em.

92

There was a young artist named Mentzel
Whose prick was as sharp as a pencil.
　　He pierced through an actress,
　　The sheet and the mattress,
And punctured the bedroom utensil.

93

A palaeontologist, Locke,
Found a fossilised Jurassic cock.
   'Is it Tyrannosaurus?
   It's huge, black and porous –
And Christ, it's still hard as a rock!'

94

There was a young lady of Twickenham
Who thought men had not enough prick in 'em.
   On her knees every day
   To God she would pray
To lengthen and strengthen and thicken 'em.

95

An old archaeologist, Throstle,
Discovered a marvellous fossil.
   He could tell from its bend
   And the knob on the end
'Twas the peter of Paul the Apostle.

96

There was a young damsel named Baker
Who was poked in a pew by a Quaker.
   He yelled, 'My God! What
   Do you call this – a twat?
Why, the entrance is more than an acre!'

97

There was an old man of Tagore
Whose tool was a yard long or more,
   So he wore the damn thing
   In a surgical sling
To keep it from wiping the floor.

98

A certain young person of Ghent,
Uncertain if lady or gent,
  Shows his organs at large
  For a small handling charge
To assist him in paying the rent.

99

There was a young lady named Brent
With a cunt of enormous extent,
  And so deep and so wide,
  The acoustics inside
Were so good you could hear when you spent.

100

There once was a Queen of Bulgaria
Whose bush had grown hairier and hairier,
  Till a prince from Peru
  Who came up for a screw
Had to hunt for her cunt with a terrier.

101

There was a young man from Stamboul
Who boasted so torrid a tool
  That each female crater
  Explored by this satyr
Seemed almost unpleasantly cool.

102

There was a young man of Coblenz
The size of whose balls was immense.
  One day, playing soccer,
  He sprung his left knocker,
And kicked it right over the fence.

103

On guard by the bridge of Carquinez
With his eyes on the evening star, Venus,
　　With the sky full of blimps,
　　And the town full of pimps,
And an incredible length in his penis.

104

There was a young lady from China
Who mistook for her mouth her vagina.
　　Her clitoris huge
　　She covered with rouge
And lipsticked her labia minor.

105

There once was a gouty old colonel
Who grew glum when the weather grew vernal,
　　And he cried in his tiffen
　　For his prick wouldn't stiffen,
And the *size* of the thing was infernal.

106

There was a young fellow of Harrow
Whose john was the size of a marrow.
　　He said to his tart,
　　'How's this for a start?
My balls are outside in a barrow.'

Satin and Lace
(and other lovely sights)

❦

1

There was a young lady named Grimes
Who spent all her nickels and dimes
 On satin and lace
 To hold her in place
And keep her abreast of the times.

2

Pearl's panties came down with a jerk,
As she bared her fair bottom for work.
 Said she, 'Pants are silly,
 But the men like them frilly,
And chewing them drives men berserk.'

3

There was a young lady of Chichester,
Whose curves made the saints in their niches stir.
 One morning at matins
 Her breasts in rose satins
Made the Bishop of Chichester's breeches stir.

4

There once was a monk of Camyre
Who was seized with a carnal desire,
 And the primary cause
 Was the abbess's drawers
Which were hung up to dry by the fire.

5

A fellow with passions quite gingery
Was exploring his young sister's lingerie;
    Then with giggles of pleasure
    He plundered her treasure,
Adding incest to insult and injury.

6

A young man with passions quite gingery
Tore a hole in his sister's lingerie;
    He slapped her behind
    And made up his mind
To add incest to insult and injury.

7

The excitement produced by Miss Whipple
Was very much more than a ripple.
    She was covered in clothes
    From her head to her toes
Save for delicate holes at each nipple.

8

An eclectic young cleric named Casey
Favours underthings pink, silk and lacy.
    Though his vows are quite strict
    They don't seem to conflict
With his sex life, both DC and AC.

9

There was a plump girl from Bryn Mawr
Who committed a dreadful *faux pas*;
    She loosened a stay
    On her *décolleté*,
Thus exposing her *je ne sais quoi*.

10

A girl while attending Bryn Mawr
Was pinched by her low strapless bra;
   She loosened one wire –
   Whereupon the entire
Dress fell, and left her quite raw.

11

A bather in Lake Ballyclear
Had a bust that would burst a brassière;
   She had a round face,
   And was plump everyplace,
Except for her flat-chested rear.

12

A concert conductor in Rio
Fell in love with a lady called Cleo;
   As she took down her panties,
   He said: 'No *andantes*!
I want it *allegro con brio*!'

13

A vigorous fellow named Bert
Was attracted by every new skirt –
   Oh, it wasn't their minds
   But their rounded behinds
That excited this lovable flirt.

14

As Mozart composed a sonata
The maid bent to fasten her garter;
   Without any delay
   He started to play
Un poco piu appassionata.

15

The *derrière* Carrie displays
Never fails to delight and amaze.
She puts every ounce
Into use, with a bounce!
And her boyfriend's ecstatic for days.

16

The pantyhose style is first-class
For revealing the shapely young lass.
    All the better to view her,
    But damn hard to screw her,
With those stockings up over her ass!

17

There was a young lady of Bude,
Who walked down the street in the nude.
    A policeman said, 'Whatumm
    Magnificent bottom!'
And slapped it as hard as hard as he could.

18

Every time Lady Lowbodice swoons,
Her bubbies pop out like balloons;
    But her butler stands by
    With hauteur in his eye
And lifts them back in with warm spoons.

19

There's a singer in Long Island City
Whose form is impressively pretty;
    She is often addressed
    By the name of 'Beau Chest',
Which is thought to be tasteful and witty.

20

A corpulent lady named Kroll
Had an idea exceedingly droll:
   She went to a ball
   Dressed in nothing at all
And backed in as a Parker House roll.

21

There are some things we mustn't expose
So we hide them away in our clothes.
   Oh, it's shocking to stare
   At what's certainly there –
But why this is so, heaven knows.

22

There is a sad rumour that Mona
Goes around in a black net kimona.
   Don't think for a minute
   There's anything in it –
Anything much besides Mona.

23

Said a calendar model named Gloria,
'So the men can enjoy real euphoria,
   You pose as you are,
   In Jan, Feb and Mar,
Then in April they want to see Moria!

24

There was a young lady of Spain
Who took down her pants on the train.
   There was a young porter
   Saw more than he orter
And asked her to do it again.

25

There was a young lady named Eva
Who went to a ball as Godiva.
　　But a change in the lights
　　Showed a tear in her tights,
And a low fellow present yelled, 'Beaver!'

26

'It's my custom,' said dear Lady Norris,
'To beg lifts from the drivers of lorries.
　　When they get out to piss
　　I see things that I miss
At the wheel of my two-seater Morris.'

27

There was a young woman named Astor
Whose clothes fitted tight as a plaster.
　　When she happened to sneeze
　　She felt a cold breeze
And knew she had met with disaster.

28

There was a young girl from Australia
Who dressed for a ball as a dahlia;
　　When the petals uncurled
　　They revealed to the world
That the dress as a dress was a failure.

29

A girl who was from Brooklyn Heights
Looked quite mediocre in tights.
　　There was much more approval
　　When upon their removal
She revealed more spectacular sights.

30

There was a young lady of Tottenham,
Her manners – she'd completely forgotten 'em;
   While at tea at the vicar's,
   She took off her knickers,
Explaining she felt much too hot in 'em.

31

Exuberant Sue from Anjou
Found that sex always altered her hue.
   She presented to sight
   Some parts pink, some parts white,
And others quite purple and blue.

32

I love her in her evening gown,
I love her in her nightie,
   But when moonlight flits
   Between her tits,
Jesus Christ, almighty!

33

Said a luscious young lady called Wade,
On a beach with her charms all displayed:
   'It's so hot in the sun,
   Perhaps rape would be fun,
At least that would give me some shade.'

34

There was a young man of Bulgaria
Who once went to piss down an area.
   Said Mary to cook,
   'Oh, do come and look,
Did you ever see anything hairier?'

35

A tall rugger blue, up from Strood,
Strode along King's Parade in the nude.
    An old don said, 'What a m
    Agnificent bottom!'
And smacked it, as hard as he could!

36

Said a chic and attractive young Greek,
'Would you like a quick peek that's unique?'
    'Why, yes,' Joe confessed,
    So she quickly undressed
And showed him her sleek Greek physique.

37

Some bird-watchers through their field-glasses
See flashes of heaving, bare arses.
    Now do you see why,
    Though bloodshot of eye,
Bird-watching appeals to the masses?

38

There was a young woman from Aenos
Who came to our party as Venus.
    We told her how rude
    'Twas to come there quite nude,
And we brought her a leaf from the greenh'use.

39

There was a young girl of Eau Claire
Who once was attacked by a bear.
    While chased in a field
    She tripped and revealed
Some meat to the bear that was rare.

40

The peach fuzz of young Miss McSweeney
Curls out from her teeny bikini:
   It's a glorious sight
   To be viewed with delight
And it stirs even grandpappy's wienie.

41

There once was a maid with such graces
That her curves cried aloud for embraces.
   'You look,' said McGee,
   'Like a million to me –
Invested in all the right places.'

42

There was a young lady called Etta,
Who fancied herself in a sweater;
   Three reasons she had:
   Keeping warm was not bad,
But the other two reasons were better.

43

A lady who rules Fort Montgomery
Says the wearing of clothes is a mummery;
   She has frequently tea'd in
   The costume of Eden,
Appearing delightfully summery.

44

A senorita who strolled on the Corso
Displayed quite a lot of her torso.
   A crowd soon collected
   And no one objected,
Though some were in favour of more so.

47

There was a young fellow named Chick
Who fancied himself rather slick.
    He went to a ball
    Dressed in nothing at all
But a big velvet bow round his prick.

48

A lady athletic and handsome
Got wedged in her sleeping-room transom.
    When she offered much gold
    For release, she was told
That the view was worth more than the ransom.

49

There was a young girl of Llewellyn
Whose breasts were as big as a melon.
    They were big, it is true,
    But her cunt was big too,
Like a bifocal, full-colour, aerial view
Of Cape Horn and the Straits of Magellan.

50

Alas for the Countess d'Isère,
Whose muff wasn't furnished with hair;
    Said the Count, '*Quelle surprise!*'
    When he parted her thighs;
'*Magnifique! Pourtant pas de la guerre.*'

Disappointments

❦

1

What's reddish and roundish and hairy,
And hangs from a bush light and airy;
   Much hidden away
   From the broad light of day
Beneath a stiff prick? A gooseberry!

2

There was a young lady of Worcester
Who dreamt that a rooster seduced her.
   She woke with a scream,
   But 'twas only a dream
A lump in the mattress had goosed her.

3

Her husband is in the Hussars,
A colonel, all covered with scars;
   But it isn't his weals
   For which nightly she feels,
But the privates he lost in the wars.

4

An unfortunate lad from Madrid
Had both Super-Ego and Id,
   So whether he screwed
   Or completely eschewed
He felt guilty, whatever he did.

5

There was a young fellow named Bliss
Whose sex life was strangely amiss.
  For even with Venus
  His recalcitrant penis
Would seldom do better than t

                                        h
                                        i
                                        s.

6

Cried her partner, 'My dear Lady Schmoosing,
While I'll own that stinkfinger's amusing,
  Still, this constant delay
  Tends to hold up the play,
And this goom on the deck's most confusing.'

7

There was a young lady from Kincaid
Who covered it up with a band-aid.
  The boyfriend said, 'Shit,
  I can't find the slit!'
And helped himself out with a hand-aid.

8

There was a young man of Kutki
Who could blink himself off with one eye.
  For a while though, he pined,
  When his organ declined
To function, because of a stye.

9

There was a young man from Purdue
Who was only just learning to screw,
  But he hadn't the knack,
  And he got too far back –
In the right church, but in the wrong pew.

10

There was an old phoney named Kinsey
Whose ideas of fucking were flimsy.
  He knew how to measure
  A penis for pleasure,
But he came much too quick in a quim, see?

11

There once was a Swede in Minneapolis,
Discovered his sex life was hapless:
  The more he would screw
  The more he'd want to,
And he feared he would soon be quite sapless.

12

There was a young fellow from Parma
Who was solemnly screwing his charmer.
  Said the damsel, demure,
  'You'll excuse me, I'm sure,
But I *must* say you fuck like a farmer.'

13

A water-pipe suited Miss Hunt,
Who used it for many a bunt,
  But the unlucky wench
  Got it caught in her trench –
It took twenty-two men and a big Stillson wrench
    to get the thing out of her cunt.

14

There were three young ladies of Fetters,
Annoyed all their elders and betters
  By stuffing their cock-holders
  With proxies for stockholders,
Old bills and anonymous letters.

15

As Apollo was chasing the fair
Daphne, she vanished in air.
   He could find but a shrub
   With thick bark on the hub
And not even a knot-hole to spare.

16

There was a young man from Bengal
Who got in a hole in the wall.
   'Oh,' he said, 'it's a pity
   This hole is so glitty,
But it's better than nothing at all.'

17

A daring young maid from Dubuque
Risked a rather decided rebuke
   By receiving a prude
   In the absolute nude,
But he gasped, 'If you only could cook!'

18

As dull as the life of the cloister
(Except it's a little bit moister)
   Mutatis mutandum
   Non est disputandum
There's no thrill in sex for the oyster.

19

There was an old fellow of Michigan
Who said, 'Oh, I wish I were rich again.
   But when I'm ahead
   I fall into the bed
Of that rotten old gold-digging bitch again.'

20

On May Day the girls of Penzance,
Being bored by a lack of romance,
  Joined the workers' parade
  With this banner displayed:
'What the Pants of Penzance Need Is Ants.'

21

There was a young man of Bombay
Who fashioned a cunt out of clay,
  But the heat of his prick
  Turned it into a brick,
And chafed all his foreskin away.

22

Full ninety years old was friend Wynn
When he went to a hookshop to sin.
  But try as he would
  It did him no good.
For all he had left was the skin.

23

There was a young fairy named Lessing
Whose fastidiousness was distressing;
  He met many a lad
  Who could have been had
But found their prepuces unprepossessing.

24

A miner who bored in Brazil
Found some very strange rust on his drill.
  He thought it a joke
  Till the bloody thing broke –
Now his tailings are practically nil.

25

There was a young man of Kildare,
Who was having a girl in a chair.
  At the sixty-third stroke
  The furniture broke,
And his rifle went off in the air.

26

There was a young girl of Pitlochry,
Who was had by a man in a rockery.
  She said: 'Oh! You've come
  All over my bum;
This isn't a fuck – it's a mockery.'

27

There was a young man named Hughes
Who swore off all kinds of booze.
  He said, 'When I'm muddled
  My senses get fuddled
And I pass up too many screws.'

28

A young Juliet of St Louis
On a balcony stood, acting screwy.
  Her Romeo climbed,
  But he wasn't well timed,
And half-way up, off he went – blooey!

29

A philosopher known for sarcasm
Took a lass to his bed for orgasm,
  But found, to his shock,
  He had a limp cock,
And dismissed her as nothing but phantasm.

30

Said an unhappy female named Sears,
'The world seems just full of those queers!
    At parties I go to
    Are no men to say "no" to;
They swish about, waggling their rears.'

31

There was a young lady named Meyer
Whose hemlines got higher and higher;
    But the size of her thighs
    Provoked merely surprise,
And extinguished the flames of desire.

32

There was a young soldier from Munich
Whose penis hung down past his tunic;
    And their chops girls would lick
    When they thought of his prick:
But alas! he was only a eunuch.

33

When Lazarus came back from the dead
He still couldn't function in bed.
    'What good's Resurrection
    Without an erection?'
Old Lazarus testily said.

34

There was a young fellow named Goody
Who claimed that he wouldn't; but would he?
    If he found himself nude
    With a girl in the nude,
The question's not would he? but could he?

35

There was a young man of Beirut
Played a penis as one might a flute,
  Till he met a sad eunuch
  Who lifted his tunic
And said, 'Sir, my instrument's mute.'

36

The life of a clerk of the session
Was strangled in psychic repression,
  But his maladies ceased
  When his penis uncreased
In straight geometric progression.

37

'For the tenth time, dull Daphnis,' said Chloë,
'You've told me my bosom is snowy.
  You have made much fine verse on
  Each part of my person.
Now DO something, there's a good boy.'

38

There was a young lady of Brabant
Who slept with an impotent savant.
  She admitted, 'We shouldn't,
  But it turned out he couldn't;
So you can't say we have when we haven't!'

39

Consider the Emperor Nero –
Of many lewd tales he's the hero –
  Though he scraped on the fiddle,
  He just couldn't diddle –
And his *real* batting average was zero.

40

A handsome young monk in a wood
Told a girl she should cling to the good.
   She obeyed him, but gladly,
   He repulsed her, but sadly,
And said she had misunderstood.

41

Her limp lover Maud couldn't pardon
He was no use at all in the garden;
   But drooped like the rose
   When the sap in it goes.
' 'Ere, Enoch,' she cried, 'Enoch, 'arden!'

42

There was a young fellow named Fyfe
Who married the pride of his life;
   But imagine his pain
   When he struggled in vain
And just couldn't get into his wife.

43

There once was a young man named Murray
Who made love to his girl in a surrey.
   She started to sigh
   But someone came by
So he fastened his pants in a hurry.

44

There once was duchess named Sally
Who led her young page up an alley.
   She was quite out of luck,
   For the lad wouldn't fuck,
And she muttered, 'How green was my valet!'

45

Petunia, the prude of Mount Hood,
Devised an odd object of wood
   Which, employed on hot nights,
   Gave her carnal delights
Far beyond what the average man could.

46

There was a young girl whose frigidity
Approached cataleptic rigidity –
   Till you gave her a drink
   When she quickly would sink
To a state of complaisant liquidity.

47

There was a young man up in Utah
Who constructed a condom of pewter.
   He said, 'I confess
   You feel nothing – or less,
But it makes you as safe as a neuter.'

48

It somehow seems highly ironical
That a Londoner laid Miss McGonagal,
   And having no rubber
   The sex-crazy lubber
Whipped out and inserted his monocle!

49

Ah, Vienna, the fortress of Freud!
Whose surgeons are always employed;
   Where boys with soft hands
   Are provided with glands
And two-fisted girls are de-boyed.

50

A girl by the green Susquehanna
Said she would do it *mañana*,
  But her lover got sore
  And sailed off to Ladore . . .
And now she must use a banana.

51

An athletic young fellow in Venice
Got the stone from straining at tennis.
  When his jock wouldn't stand
  She who had it in hand
Said, 'These out-door sports are a menace.'

52

There once was a eunuch of Roylem,
Took two eggs to the cook and said, 'Boil 'em.
  I'll sling 'em beneath
  My inadequate sheath,
And slip into the harem and foil 'em.'

53

A sex-mad young gay boy named Willie
Whose antics are frequently silly,
  Has had, just for fun,
  A vasectomy done –
An instance of 'gelding the lily'.

54

A lad, grown too tight, one supposes,
Was dreadfully sore with phimosis.
  The doctor said, 'Why,
  Circumcision we'll try –
A plan recommended by Moses.'

55

There was a young girl of Mobile
Whose hymen was made of chilled steel.
   To give her a thrill
   Took a rotary drill
Or a Number 9 emery wheel.

56

There was a young man from Calcutta
Who was heard in his beard to mutter,
   'If her Bartholin glands
   Don't respond to my hands,
I'm afraid I shall have to use butter.'

57

A nervous young fellow named Fred
Took a charming young widow to bed.
   When he'd diddled a while
   She remarked with a smile,
'You've got it all in but the head.'

58

There was a young fellow called Simon
Who for years couldn't pierce his wife's hymen,
   Till he hit on the trick
   Of sheathing his prick
In a steel condom studded with diamond.

59

The eminent Dr Barnard
Has called it 'a baseless *canard*'
   That injecting epoxy
   In older men's cocks he
Has caused them again to get hard.

60

There was a young man from Vancouver
Whose existence had lost its prime mover.
  But its loss he supplied
  With a piece of bull's hide,
Two pears, and the bag from the Hoover.

61

A bobby from Effingham Junction,
Whose organ had long ceased to function,
  Deceived his good wife,
  For the rest of her life
With the aid of his constable's truncheon.

62

There was a young man from Seattle
Whose testicles tended to rattle.
  He said as he fucked
  Some stones in a bucket,
'If Stravinsky won't deafen you, that'll.'

63

In Utrecht the great Dr Strabismus
Found his bride had acute vaginismus.
  His very first fuck,
  He found himself stuck,
And had to stay in her till Christmas.

64

There was a young fellow of Burma
Whose betrothed had good reason to murmur;
  But now that he's married he's
  Using cantharides
And the root of their love is much firmer.

65

There was a young lady in Brent,
When her old man's pecker it bent,
   She said with a sigh,
   'Oh, why must it die?
Let's fill it with Portland cement.'

66

There was an old man of Decatur
Took out his red-hot pertater.
   He tried at her dent,
   But when his thing bent,
He got down on his knees and he ate 'er.

67

A young man, of his fate in defiance,
Took advantage of prosthetic science.
   His manhood was lost
   (The result of whore-frost),
So he fucked with a plastic appliance.

68

There was a young lady of Chiswick,
Who consulted a doctor of physic;
   He tested her hormones,
   And sexual performones,
Then prescribed her a strong aphrodisic.

69

A geologist named Dr Robb
Was perturbed by his thingamybob,
   So he took up his pick
   And whanged off his wick,
And calmly went on with his job.

70

Have you heard of Professor MacKay
Who lays all the girls in the hay?
   Though he thinks it's romantic
   He drives them all frantic
By *talking* a wonderful lay.

71

A girl of as graceful a mien
As ever in London was seen,
   Stepped into a pub,
   Hit her man with a club,
And razored to shreds his machine.

72

All winter the eunuch from Munich
Went out wearing only his tunic.
   Folk said, 'You've a cough:
   You'll freeze your balls off!'
Said he, 'I'm already a eunuch.'

73

My sex life is pretty humdrum:
When I'm ready and want George to plumb,
   He says, 'Wait a minute,
   I've hardly got in it' –
Then before I begin it, he's come.

74

In bed, the Romantics were vile
(Lord Byron apart). Shelley's style
   Was to lick his wife's belly,
   While poor Mary Shelley
Wrote *Frankenstein*, grimly, meanwhile.

75

There was a young man of Natal,
Who was having a Hottentot gal.
  She said: 'Oh, you sluggard!'
  He said: 'You be buggered!
I like to fuck slow, and I shall.'

76

There was a young lad from Nahant
Who was made like the Sensitive Plant.
  When asked, 'Do you fuck?'
  He replied, 'No such luck.
I would if I could but I can't.'

77

Said a lecherous fellow named Shea,
When his prick wouldn't rise for a lay,
  'You must seize it, and squeeze it,
  And tease it, and please it,
for Rome wasn't built in a day.'

78

'Well, I took your advice, doc,' said Knopp.
'Told my wife she'd like it on top.
  She bounced for an hour
  Till she ran out of power
And the kids, who got bored, made her stop.'

79

There was a young miss from St Simon,
Who sighed to her gentleman, 'Why, man,
  I've torn underwear,
  And you've rubbed off the hair,
But you haven't yet punctured my hymen!'

80

There was a young fellow named Phil
Who was screwing a girl, as boys will.
   She had a girl's knack
   Of screwing right back:
The instinct's not easy to kill.

81

A 'brickie' who had a fine tool
Was thought by his girlfriend too cool,
   For when he was up her,
   He broke for a cuppa –
As that was his union rule.

82

There was a young lady of Ealing
And her lover before her was kneeling.
   Said she, 'Dearest Jim,
   Take you hand off my quim;
I much prefer fucking to feeling.'

83

When the Bermondsey bricklayers struck,
Bill Bloggins was 'aving a fuck,
   By union rules
   He 'ad to down tools –
Now wasn't that bloody 'ard luck!

84

There once was a girl at the Ritz
Who liked to have men bite her tits.
   One good Fletcherizer
   Made her sadder but wiser
By chewing them up into bits.

85

The Shah of the Empire of Persia
Lay for days in a sexual merger.
 When the nautch asked the Shah,
 'Won't you ever withdraw?'
He replied, 'It's not love; it's inertia.'

86

There was a young man from Mobile
Who wondered just how it would feel
 To carry a gong
 Hanging down from his dong,
And occasionally let the thing peal.

So he rigged up a clever device,
And tried the thing out once or twice,
 But it wasn't the gong
 But rather his prong
That peeled, and it didn't feel nice!

87

There was a young fellow named Dick
Who was cursed with a spiralling prick,
 So he set out to hunt
 For a screw-twisted cunt
That would match with his corkscrewy dick.

He found one, and took it to bed,
And then in chagrin he dropped dead,
 For that spiralling snatch
 It never would match –
The damn thing had a left-handed thread!

Consequences: Babies and Blisters

❦

1

It seems I impregnated Marge,
So I do rather feel, by and large,
   Some dough should be tendered
   For services rendered,
But I can't quite decide what to charge.

2

Making love is no longer a thrill
When my girl keeps forgetting her pill.
   The hours seem myriad
   Awaiting her period –
If she misses, I'm off to Brazil!

3

There was a young lady named Flo
Whose lover was almighty slow.
   So they tried it all night
   Till he got it just right,
For practice makes pregnant, you know.

4

Said an ape, as he swung by his tail,
To his offspring both female and male:
   'From *your* offspring, my dears,
   In a couple of years,
May evolve a professor at Yale.'

5

Three lovely girls from St Thomas
Attended dance halls in pyjamas.
  They were fondled all summer
  By bass, sax and drummer –
I'm surprised that by now they're not mamas.

6

A free-loving damsel named Hall
Once went to a birth-control ball.
  She took an appliance
  To make love with science
But nobody asked her at all.

7

A naïve teenager, Miss Lewis,
Asked, 'What is it fellows do to us
  That makes babies come –
  Or am I just dumb?'
Her sister's reply was, 'They screw us.'

8

When Dick made a young lady from Clare,
He was the very first one to get there.
  She said, 'Copulation
  Can result in gestation,
But gosh, now you're there, I don't care.'

9

There was a young lady of Delhi
Who had a bad pain in her belly.
  Her relations all smiled
  'Cos they found her with child
By his honour the C—f B—n K—y.

10

To evade paternity, Mick
Said, 'Anal or oral, you pick.
  Try sucking my cock
  It's like Blackpool rock.
Oh, come on, just give it a lick.'

11

A husband who craved to be sterile,
Because of the pregnancy peril,
  Said, 'I've thought of vasectomy,
  But my wife then might hector me
And threaten divorce when we quarrel.'

12

In the sea Puerto Rico's a cork;
Its national bird is the stork.
  The natives deploy
  To share natural joy,
And export the results to New York.

13

In spring, Miss May marries Perce,
Till then their pash' they disburse:
  With a thin piece of rubber
  There's no need to scrub 'er –
Of course, there's no harm to rehearse.

14

There was a young man of Penzance
Who rogered his three maiden aunts.
  Though them he defiled,
  He never got them with child,
Through using the letters of France.

15

There was a young girl of Bombay
Who was put in the family way
　　By the mate of a lugger,
　　An ignorant bugger
Who always spelled cunt with a k.

16

There was a young man of Cape Cod
Who once put my wife into pod.
　　His name it was Tucker
　　The dirty old fucker,
The bugger, the blighter, the sod!

17

Said a prudish young person named Reed,
'The gross way that we humans breed
　　Viewed coldly, looks frightful,
　　Though I'm told it's delightful;
So, if you don't mind, let's proceed.'

18

Said Einstein, 'I have an equation
Which science might call Rabelaisian.
　　Let P be virginity
　　Approaching infinity
And U be a constant, persuasion.

Now, if P over U be inverted
And the square root of U be inserted
　　X times over P
　　The result, QED,
Is a relative,' Einstein asserted.

19

The world population's a fright:
The number's soared right out of sight.
   Who's to blame – bear the brunt?
   Why, the cock and the cunt,
And expense of electric light.

20

There was a young lady called Starky
Who had an affair with a darky;
   The result of her sins
   Was quads and not twins:
One white and one black, and two khaki.

21

There was a young monk from Siberia
Whose morals were very inferior;
   He did to a nun
   What he shouldn't have done,
And now she's a Mother Superior.

22

A young girl, imprudent and errant,
Did things that more cautious girls daren't.
   She hoped and expected
   To go undetected,
But is slowly becoming ap-parent.

23

There was a young lady named Sue
Who preferred a stiff drink to a screw.
   But one leads to the other,
   And now she's a mother –
Let this be a lesson to you.

24

There was a young lady of Perth
Who said, 'Lord! I'm increasing in girth!'
   And her lovely young figure
   Grew steadily bigger
And bigger – till after the birth.

25

A well-poised young lady named Sawyer
Claimed nothing could vex or annoy her.
   But the baby I fathered
   Had her hot and bothered
And I get nasty calls from her lawyer.

26

There was a young lady of Maine
Who declared she'd a man on the brain.
   But you knew from the view
   Of her waist, as it grew,
It was not on her brain that he'd lain.

27

You will read in Professor Schmunk's treatise,
In the words of the famed Epictetus,
   The curious lore
   That young girls by the score
Are afflicted with athlete's foetus.

28

There was a young girl of Cape Cod
Who thought babies were fashioned by God;
   But 'twas not the Almighty
   Who hiked up her nightie
But Roger the lodger – the sod!

29

There was a young wife who begat
Three husky boys, Nat, Pat and Tat.
    They all yelled for food,
    And a problem ensued
When she found there was no tit for tat.

30

A round-the-world traveller named Ann
Took up with a Tokyo man.
    The relationship thrived
    And her baby arrived
With its bottom stamped MADE IN JAPAN.

31

There was a young girl of Penzance
Who decided to take just one chance;
    She let herself go
    On the lap of her beau
And now all her sisters are aunts.

32

Said my wife as she stood on a rostrum,
'I don't mind if I don't have colostrum,
    But I'll take an option
    If your child's for adoption –
Though I cannot bear kids, I can foster 'em.'

33

Young girls of seductive proportions
Should take contraceptive precautions.
    Silly young Ermyntrude
    Let one small sperm intrude . . .
Who's the best man for abortions?

34

An innocent girl once said, 'Lumme, m'm!
I shall soon an unmarried mum become:
　　Lord, yes! it was fun
　　When we did what we done,
But he lied when he called it a dummy run.'

35

There once was a virgin named Claire
Who would do anything for a dare.
　　But one dare, she found,
　　Made her tummy grow round,
And she now has a visitor there.

36

A surly and pessimist Druid,
A defeatist, if only he knew it,
　　Said, 'The world's on the skids
　　And I think having kids
Is a waste of good seminal fluid.'

37

There was a young girl of Lapland
Whose belly began to expand.
　　She cried, 'It's a baby!'
　　Her boyfriend said, 'Maybe –
From now on, we'll do it by hand.'

38

An ignorant maiden named Rewdid
Did something amazingly stupid:
　　When her lover had spent
　　She douched with cement
And gave birth to a statue of Cupid.

39

There was a young girl from Madrid
Who learned she was having a kid.
   By holding her water
   Two months and a quarter
She drowned the poor bastard, she did.

40

A prolific young mother named Hall
Who seemed to have triplets each fall,
   When asked why and wherefore,
   Said, 'That's what we're here for,
But we often get nothing at all.'

41

Artificial insemination
Some say will replace fornication;
   But perish the day
   When the old-fashioned way
Can't supply enough kids for the nation!

42

Said an ovum one night to a sperm,
'You're a very attractive young germ!
   Come join me, my sweet,
   Let our nuclei meet
And in nine months we'll both come to term.'

43

There was a young girl of Milpitas
Exceptionally fond of coitus,
   Till a half-back from State
   Made her periods late –
A sure case of athlete's foetus.

44

There was a young lady of Wantage
Of whom the town clerk took advantage.
　　Said the county surveyor,
　　'Of course you must pay her;
You've altered the line of her frontage.'

45

There was a young bride, a Canuck,
Told her husband, 'Let's do more than suck.
　　You say that I, maybe,
　　Can have my first baby –
Let's give up this Frenching, and fuck!'

46

Alack, for the doughty O'Connor
Who fucked like a fiend for his honour.
　　Till a flapper named Rhea
　　Colluded to be a
Mother to Leuco and Gonor.

47

An indolent vicar of Bray
Kept his wife in the family way,
　　Till she grew more alert,
　　Bought a vaginal squirt,
And said to her spouse, 'Let us spray!'

48

There was a young lady of Michigan
Who said, 'Damn it! I've got the itch again.'
　　Said her mother, 'That's strange,
　　I'm surprised it ain't mange,
If you've slept with that son-of-a-bitch again.'

49

Though the practice of young Heloise is
To pleasure whomever she pleases,
    She admits the one hitch is
    She suffers from itches
And various social diseases.

50

There's a girl there on Marathon Key
Who gave my pal Flip the VD.
    Evil ways are a curse.
    Still, it might have been worse –
Had I called 'heads' it would have been me!

51

There was a young fellow named Pfister
Who noticed an odd sort of blister
    Where no blister should be
    What was worse, do you see,
He had got it at home from his sister.

52

There was an old man of Goditch,
Had the syph and the clap and the itch.
    His name was McNabs
    And he also had crabs,
The dirty old son of a bitch.

53

There was a young rounder named Fisk
Whose method of screwing was brisk.
    And his reason was: 'If
    The damned bitch has the syph,
This way I'm reducing the risk.'

54

Berries, berries, all kinds of berries,
Chancres on her ass like California cherries.
     The first time I hit her
     I nearly broke her shitter,
Down where the Hasiampa flows.

55

There was a young girl from Mauritius,
Who said, 'That last bit was delicious.
     But if you don't mind,
     We'll postpone the next grind,
As that spot on your tool looks suspicious.'

56

There's a man in the city of Dublin
Whose pego is always him troubling,
     And it's now come to this,
     That he can't go to piss,
But the spunk with the piddle comes bubbling.

57

There was a young woman of Chester
Who said to the man who undressed her,
     'I think you will find
     That it's better behind –
The front is beginning to fester.'

58

There was a young woman of Cheadle
Who once gave the clap to a beadle.
     Said she, 'Does it itch?'
     'It does, you damned bitch,
And burns like hell-fire when I peedle.'

59

There was a young man of Cashmere
Who purchased a fine Bayadere.
    He fucked all her toes,
    Her mouth, eyes, and her nose,
And eventually poxed her left ear.

60

A president called Gambetta
Once used an imperfect french letter.
    This was not the worst,
    With disease he got cursed,
And he took a long time to get better.

61

There was an old party of Fife
Who suspected a clap in his wife.
    So he bought an injection
    To cure the infection,
Which gave him a stricture for life.

62

He'll be there to inspect me,
With a big syringe to inject me –
    Oh, I'll be humpbacked
    Before I get back
To Ten–Ten–Tennessee . . .

63

There was a young lady of Gaza
Who shaved her cunt clean with a razor.
    The crabs in a lump
    Made tracks to her rump,
Which proceeding did greatly amaze her.

64

A rank whore, there ne'er was a ranker,
Possessed an Hunterian chancre,
 But she made an elision
 By a transverse incision,
For which all her lovers may thank her.

65

There was a young lady named Hitchin
Who was scratching her crotch in the kitchen.
 Her mother said, 'Rose,
 It's the crabs, I suppose.'
She said, 'Yes, and the buggers are itchin'.'

66

There was a young woman of Hadley
Who would with an omnibus cad lie.
 He gave her the crabs,
 And besides minor scabs
The pox too she got very badly.

67

There was a young maid of Klepper
Went out one night with a stepper,
 And now in dismay
 She murmurs each day,
'His pee-pee was made of red-pepper!'

68

A rosy-cheeked lass from Dunellen,
Whom the Hoboken sailors call Helen,
 In her efforts to please
 Has spread social disease
From New York to the Straits of Magellan.

69

There was a young lady at sea
Who complained that it hurt her to pee.'
  'Indeed?' said the mate.
  'That accounts for the state
Of the captain, the purser and me.'

70

Said the Earl to the Countess of Cottam
(Who had crabs, but knew not where she'd got 'em):
  'My dear, you're too generous
  With your *mons Veneris*
And equally so with your bottom.'

71

Remember those two of Aberystwyth
Who connected the things that they pissed with?
  She sat on his lap
  But they both had the clap
And they cursed with the things that they kissed with.

72

There was a young girl of Bavaria
Who thought her disease was malaria.
  But the family doc
  Explained to her shock,
'It began in your genital area.'

73

There was a young lecher named Trapp
Who thought using condoms was crap.
  Said he, 'Us real he-men
  Like to scatter our semen!'
Six months later, he still has the clap.

74

On a business trip to DC,
Jack picked up a case of VD.
   For ten bucks a shot
   He was saved from cock rot,
And lives now in celibacy.

75

A worried teenager from Poole
Discovered red spots on his tool.
   Said the doctor, a cynic,
   'Get out of my clinic.
Just wipe off the lipstick, you fool!'

76

There once was a doughty Norwegian
Who enlivened the French Foreign Legion;
   But his brothers-in-arms
   Who succumbed to his charms
Got the clap in their hindermost region.

77

There was a young girl of Uttoxeter,
And all the young men shook their cocks at her.
   From one of these cocks
   She contracted the pox,
And she poxed all the cocks in Uttoxeter.

78

There was an old man of Molucca
Who wanted his daughter, to fuck her.
   But she got the best
   Of his little incest,
And poxed the old man of Molucca.

79

There was a young girl named Maxine
Whose vagina was wondrously clean:
    With her uterus packed
    She kept safe from attack
With a dill pickle, papulous, green.

80

The spouse of a pretty young thing,
Came home from the wars in the spring.
    He was lame but he came
    With his dame like a flame –
A discharge is a wonderful thing.

81

There was a young man known as Royce
Who took an emetic by choice.
    He was fed, quite by chance,
    Half the crotch of the pants
Of a girl who kept crab-lice as toys.

82

The wife of a Viking in Norway
Was caught taking a nap in a doorway.
    'When you make the attack,
    Let it be from the back,
Because lately the front way's the sore way.'

83

There was a young lady of Yap
Who had pimples all over her map.
    But in her interstices
    There lurked a far worse disease,
Commonly known as the clap.

84

A horny young soldier named Frank
Had only his girlfriend to thank
   That he didn't catch clap,
   Gonorrhoea or pap,
And wind up in an oxygen tank

85

A girl to the druggist did say,
'I am bothered with bugs in my hay.'
   'I see what you mean,
   You need Paris green
To be rid of the things right away.'

The results of this piece of mischance
Were disastrous, you'll see at a glance.
   First died bugs, then went trees,
   Then her pet Pekinese,
And two gentlemen just in from France.

86

There was a young man of Canute
Who was troubled by warts on his root.
   He put acid on these,
   And now, when he pees,
He can finger his root like a flute.

87

There was a young girl of high station
Who ruined her fine reputation
   When she said she'd the pox
   From sucking on cocks –
She should really have called it 'fellation'.

Piety

❧

1

There once was a chaplain of King's
Whose mind dwelt on heavenly things
    But his heart was on fire
    For a boy in the choir,
With a bottom like jelly on springs.

2

From the depths of the crypt at St Giles
Came a scream that resounded for miles.
    Said the vicar, 'Good gracious!
    Has Father Ignatius
Forgotten the bishop has piles?'

3

A divine by the name of McWhinners
Held classes each evening for sinners,
    They were sectioned and graded
    So the very de-graded
Would not be held back by beginners.

4

A young nun who wrote verse in her diary,
That was terribly torrid and fiery,
    Once left it behind
    For the abbess to find
Now she isn't allowed in the priory.

5

There were two young ladies of Birmingham
And this is the story concerning 'em:
 They lifted the frock
 And tickled the cock
Of the bishop as he was confirming 'em.

The bishop was nobody' s fool
(He'd been to a great public school);
 He took down their frillies
 And dealt with those fillies
With his twelve-inch episcopal tool.

But that didn't bother the two:
They said, as the bishop withdrew,
 'The vicar is quicker
 And thicker and slicker
And longer and stronger than you.'

Said the bishop, 'Of course, you are right.
The vicar's a man of great might;
 But though rather flash
 He lacks my panache,
And *he* can't come eight times in a night.'

6

The priest, a cocksucker named Sheen,
Is delighted their sins aren't seen.
 'Though God sees through walls,'
 Says monsignor, ' – Oh, balls!
This God stuff is simply a screen.'

7

A Sunday-school student in Mass
Soon rose to the head of the class
  By reciting quite bright
  And by sleeping at night
With his tongue up the minister's ass.

8

There was an old curate of Hestion
Who'd erect at the slightest suggestion.
  But so small was his tool
  He could scarce screw a spool,
And a cunt was quite out of the question.

9

There was a young girl of Gibraltar
Who was raped as she knelt at the altar.
  It really seems odd
  That a virtuous God
Should answer her prayers, and assault her.

10

'Given faith,' sighed the Vicar of Deneham,
'From the lusts of the flesh we might wean 'em.
  But the human soul sighs
  For a nice pair of thighs
And a little of what lies between 'em.'

11

There was a young girl from Sofia
Who succumbed to her lover's desire.
  She said, 'Sure, it's a sin;
  But now that it's in,
Could you shove it a little bit higher?'

12

Have you heard of the Bishop of Kew
Who preached with his vestments askew?
   A lady named Morgan
   Caught sight of his organ
And fainted away in her pew.

13

There was a young fellow named Sturges
Who needed a lass for his urges.
   But how could he buy
   With the price bid sky-high
By the men of the various clergies?

14

There was a young lady of Devon
Who was raped in the garden by seven
   High Anglican priests
   (Lascivious beasts):
Of such is the kingdom of heaven.

15

There once was a priest of Gibraltar
Who wrote dirty jokes in his psalter.
   An inhibited nun
   Who had read every one
Made a vow to be laid on his altar.

16

A young novice priest of Lahore
Ogled nuns in the convent galore.
   He climbed in and defiled one
   Who proved such a wild one
He stayed to defile her some more.

17

'Well, madam,' the bishop declared,
While the vicar just mumbled and stared,
  ' 'Twere better, perhaps,
  In the crypt or the apse,
Because sex in the nave must be shared.'

18

Mused the deacon, in deepest dejection,
As he passed round the box for collection:
  If it comes to the worst
  Can a curate be cursed
Or a rector be wrecked by erection?

19

There was a young lady named Lynne
Who said, 'I'm prepared to begin
  Any sort of activity
  Which suits my proclivity,
Provided it counts as a sin.'

20

A Salvation lassie named Claire
Was having her first love-affair.
  As she climbed into bed
  She reverently said,
'I wish to be opened with prayer.'

21

A renegade priest from Liberia
Whose morals were clearly inferior,
  Once did to a nun
  What he shouldn't have done
And now she's a Mother Superior.

22

A pious old lady of Worcester
Forgave all who'd ever abused her,
   But flew into a rage
   Which time could not assuage
When she thought of one cad who'd refused her.

23

When a lecherous curate of Leeds
Was discovered one day in the weeds
   Astride a young nun,
   He said, 'Christ this is fun!
Far better than telling one's beads.'

24

A hoary old monk of Regina
Once said, 'There is nothing diviner
   Than to sit in one's cell
   And let one's mind dwell
On the charms of the Virgin's vagina.'

25

A big Catholic layman named Fox
Makes his living by sucking off cocks.
   In spells of depression
   He goes to confession,
And jacks off the priest in his box.

26

There once was a nun whose divinity
Preserved her in perfect virginity,
   Till a candle, her nemesis,
   Caused parthenogenesis –
And she thinks herself one of the Trinity.

27

There was an old abbess quite shocked
To find nuns where the candles were locked.
   Said the abbess, 'You nuns
   Should behave more like guns,
And never go off till you're cocked.'

28

There was a young fellow named Baker
Who seduced a vivacious young Quaker.
   And when he had done it
   She straightened her bonnet
And said, 'I give thanks to my Maker.'

29

When Paul the Apostle lay prostrate,
And leisurely prodded his prostate,
   With pride parabolic
   His most apostolic
Appendage became an apostate.

30

A cardinal living in Rome
Had a Renaissance bath in his home.
   He could gaze at the nudes
   As he worked up his moods
In emulsions of semen and foam.

31

A horny young girl of Madras
Reclined with a monk in the grass.
   She tickled his cock
   With the end of a rock
Till it foamed like a bottle of Bass.

32

The swaggering hips of a jade
Raised the cock of a clerical blade.
　Hell-bent for his fun,
　He went home at the run,
And diddled his grandmother's maid.

33

A habit obscene and unsavory
Holds the Bishop of Wessex in slavery.
　With maniacal howls
　He deflowers young owls
Which he keeps in an underground aviary.

But the prior of Dunstan St Just,
Cunsumed with erotical lust,
　Raped the bishop's prize fowls
　(His treasured young owls)
And a little green lizard, what bust.

34

A bibulous bishop would preach
After sunning his balls on the beach.
　But his love life was ended
　By a paunch so distended
It annulled, *ipso facto*, his reach.

35

A hermit once thought his oasis
The best of all possible places;
　For it had a mirage
　In the form of a large
And affectionate female curvaceous.

36

A young female deacon named Fricker
Once had an affair with the vicar.
   She frigged him, butt-fucked him,
   Buggered and sucked him
('Twas under the influence of liquor).

37

There was a young girl from the Creek
Who had periods twice every week.
   'How very provoking,'
   Said the vicar from Woking,
'There's no time for poking, so to speak.'

38

There was a gay parson of Tooting
Whose roe he was frequently shooting,
   Till he married a lass
   With a face like my arse,
And a cunt you could put a top-boot in.

39

'The conception,' an archbishop said,
'Of a personal tempter is dead.'
   But a meek little curate
   Begged leave to demur; it
Was something he fought with in bed.

40

A deviate graduate from Trinity
Adored his sister to infinity,
   Made a pass at his mother,
   Had a thing with his brother,
And still got a first in Divinity.

41

There was a gay rector of Poole
Most deservedly proud of his tool.
  With some trifling aid
  From the curate, 'tis said,
He rogered the National School.

42

There was a young curate of Eltham
Who wouldn't fuck girls, but he felt 'em.
  In lanes he would linger
  And play at stink-finger,
And *scream* with delight when he smelt 'em.

43

There was an old Abbot of Khief
Who thought the Impenitent Thief
  Had bollocks of brass
  And an amethyst arse.
He died in this awful belief.

44

A modern monk nicknamed Augustin,
His penis a boy's bottom thrust in.
  Then said Father Ignatius,
  'Now really! Good gracious!
Your conduct is really disgusting.'

45

There was a young lady called Tucker,
And the parson he tried hard to fuck her.
  She said, 'You gay sinner,
  Instead of your dinner,
At my cunt you shall have a good suck, ah.'

46

There was an old party of Wokingham,
And his whores said he always was poking 'em,
　　But all he could do
　　Was to tongue-fuck a few,
And sniff at his fingers while roking 'em.

47

There was a young parson of Goring
Who made a small hole in the flooring.
　　He lined it all round,
　　Then lay on the ground,
And declared it was cheaper than whoring.

48

There was an old parson of Lundy,
Fell asleep in his vestry on Sunday.
　　He awoke with a scream:
　　'What, another wet dream!
This comes of not frigging since Monday.'

49

There was a young curate of Buckingham,
Who was blamed by the girls for not fucking 'em.
　　He said: 'Though my cock
　　Is as hard as a rock,
Your cunts are too slack. Put a tuck in 'em.'

50

There was a young man of Belgravia,
Who cared neither for God nor his Saviour.
　　He walked down the Strand
　　With his balls in his hand,
And was had up for indecent behaviour.

51

There was a young monk of Siberia,
Who of frigging grew weary and wearier.
  At last, with a yell,
  He burst from his cell,
And buggered the Father Superior.

52

Said the venerable Dean of St Paul's,
'Concerning them cracks in the walls –
  Do you think it would do,
  If we filled them with glue?'
The Bishop of Lincoln said: 'Balls.'

53

On a bridge sat the Bishop of Buckingham
Who was thinking of twats and of sucking them
  And watching the stunts
  Of the cunts in the punts
And the tricks of the pricks that were fucking them.

54

There was a young priest from Madrid
Who looked with lewd eyes on a kid.
  He said, 'With great joy,
  I could bugger that boy.
I'll be damned if I don't!' And he did.

55

Said the bishop one day to the abbott,
Whose instincts were just like a rabbit:
  'I know it's great fun
  To embrace a young nun –
But you mustn't get into the habit.'

56

St Peter was once heard to boast
That he'd had all the heavenly host:
   The Father, the Son,
   And then, just for fun,
The hole in the Holy Ghost.

57

A fervent young maid of Bermuda
Embraced all the doctrines of Buddha;
   But in six weeks, all told,
   She returned to the fold,
When the Anglican archbishop screwed her.

58

A preacher who went out to Bali
To change the sartorial folly
   Of the girls now admits,
   'A good pair of tits
In season can seem rather jolly.'

59

A contrite acolyte, name of Ansell,
Said, 'Last night, by mischance in the chancel,
   Lured by carnal desires
   I buggered two friars:
These sins by confession I'll cancel.'

Shocks: Major and Minor

❦

1

There was a young lady from Boston
Who thought she'd been raped in an Austin;
   But the truth is, I fear,
   She had sat on her gear,
And a pickle-truck knocked her exhaust in.

2

Said the groom to his best man, 'That's torn it!
I've been stung on the cock by a hornet,
   Right under my prepuce
   And it hurts like the deuce,
But the sting's out – the hornet's withdrawn it.'

3

Hear the sad tale of foolish young Post
Who cut off his manhood to roast.
   Said he, 'Though 'twas tasty,
   Perhaps I was hasty –
It's the slice I'll be missing the most.'

4

After lunch the Grand Duchess of Teck
Observed, 'If you'll listen one sec,
   We've found a man's tool
   In the small swimming pool.
So would all of you gentlemen check?'

5

There was a young man of Bengal
Who went to a masquerade ball
   Arrayed like a tree,
   But he failed to forsee
His abuse by the dogs in the hall.

6

He hated to sew, so young Ned
Rang the bell of his neighbour instead.
   But her husband said, 'Vi,
   When you stitched his torn fly,
There was no need to bite off the thread.'

7

He approached her with gentle affection
And a prominent out-thrust erection;
   But the love of his life
   Took a large carving knife
And . . . (*see Diagram 6: Conic Section*)

8

A lady skin-diver, a Gemini,
Encountered a monstrous anemone
   Far under the sea.
   It seized her with glee,
And ate up her *pudenda feminae*.

9

There was a young lady named Psyche
In bed with a fellow named Ike.
   Said he, 'Now don't worry,
   Or hurry or flurry,
But that ain't my prick – it's a spike.'

10

A dolly in Dallas named Alice,
Whose overworked cunt is all callous,
   Wore the foreskin away
   Of uncircumcised Ray,
Through exuberance, tightness and malice.

11

There once was a fabulous Creole
Whose prick had a wide-open pee-hole.
   This carrot so orange
   Got caught in the door-hinge
When he tried to bugger the key-hole.

12

There once was a gay young Parisian
Who screwed an appendix incision,
   And the girl of his choice
   Could hardly rejoice
At this horrible lack of precision.

13

A sea-cruising widow named La Sage
Declared that her quim needed massage.
   The ship's masseur, vile,
   Did the job with a file
And gave her a very rough passage.

14

There is a new Baron of Wokingham,
The girls say he don't care for poking 'em,
   Preferring 'Minette',
   Which is pleasant, but yet,
There is one disadvantage, his choking 'em.

15

There was a young lady called Hilda,
Who went for a walk with a builder;
    He knew that he could,
    And he should and he would,
And he did, and it bloody near killed her.

16

A lusty young woodsman of Maine
For years with no woman had lain,
    But he found sublimation
    At a high elevation
In the crotch of a pine – God, the pain!

17

I see a young lady named Kitty,
Lying down on the beach, very pretty.
    To her boyfriend she blurts,
    'Get it out, please; it hurts!
You've lain in the sand, and it's gritty.'

18

The dangers of zipping a zipper
Keep plump fellows watching that nipper,
    For the fiendish device
    Can take off a slice –
Beats a *mohel*, hands down, as a clipper.

19

There once was an amorous WAC
Who wanted a prick in her crack.
    She met up with a jerk
    Who made her do the work,
The result was a crick in her back.

20

There was an old lady of Cheadle
Who sat down in church on a needle.
  The needle, though blunt,
  Penetrated her cunt,
But was promptly removed by the beadle.

21

There was a young man of Datchet
Who cut off his prick with a hatchet,
  Then very politely
  He sent it to Whitely,
And ordered a cunt that would match it.

THE REPLY

'There is a young girl here at Vassar,
And none, for your needs, could surpass her.
  But she cannot detach it
  And much less dispatch it.
You'll still have to bach it. Alas, sir!'

22

There was an old man from Robles
Who went out to dine with some nobles.
  He would risk his life,
  And fuck the host's wife,
And now, so 'tis said, he has no balls.

23

There was a young lady of Tring
Who sat by the fire to sing.
  A piece of charcoal
  Flew up her arsehole
And burnt all the hair off her quim.

24

There was a young fellow named Pete
Liked to dance in the snow and the sleet.
　　One chilly November
　　He froze every member
And retired to monkish retreat.

25

On a picnic a Scot named McFee
Was stung in the balls by a bee.
　　He made oodles of money
　　By oozing pure honey
Each time he attempted to pee.

26

An impetuous couple named Kelly
Now go through life belly-to-belly:
　　Because in their haste
　　They used library paste
Instead of petroleum jelly.

27

Have you heard of the bow-legged Sam Guzzum,
And Samantha, his knock-kneed cousin?
　　There are some people say
　　That love finds a way,
But for Sam and Samantha it doesn't.

28

As the elevator car left our floor
Big Sue caught her teats in the door;
　　She yelled a good deal,
　　But had they been real,
She'd have yelled considerably more.

29

There was a young man of Eau Claire
Who had an affair with a bear,
But the surly old brute
With a snap of her snoot
Left him only one ball and some hair.

30

There was a young man of Bengal
Who swore he had only one ball,
But two little bitches
Unbuttoned his britches,
And found he had no balls at all.

31

There was a young lady named Rackstraw
Titillated herself with a hacksaw.
As a result of this action
She no longer has traction,
And a penis feels just like a jackstraw.

32

One evening a workman named Rawls
Fell asleep in his old overalls.
And when he woke up he
Discovered a puppy
Had bitten off one of his balls.

33

A cabin boy on a tea clipper
(A thoroughly nasty young nipper)
Plugged up his arse
With broken glass
And thus circumcised his old skipper.

34

There was a young sailor from Brighton
Who remarked to his girl, 'You're a tight one.'
   She replied, ' 'Pon my soul,
   You're in the wrong hole;
There's plenty of room in the right one.'

35

There once was a wicked old actor
Who waylaid a young girl and attacked her.
   In response to this trick
   She bit off his prick
And thus remained *virgo intacta*.

36

There was a young sailor named Bates
Who danced the fandango on skates.
   He fell on his cutlass
   Which rendered him nutless
And practically useless on dates.

37

An extremely short-kilted North Briton
Sat carelessly down on a kitten;
   But the kitten had claws
   The immediate cause
Of the Scotsman's abrupt circumcision.

38

There was a braw Scot from Loch Ness
Who bragged of his twelve-inch prowess,
   Till the Beast of the Loch
   Bit off most of his cock.
He now boasts considerably less!

39

There was a young Jew of Far Rockaway
Whose screams could be heard from a block away.
   Perceiving his error
   The rabbi in terror
Cried, 'God! I have cut his whole cock away!'

40

There was a young lady named Prentice
Who was ravished one day by her dentist.
   To make the thing easier
   He used anaesthesia
And drilled her *non compos mentis*.

41

There was a young lady of Ypres
Who was shot in the ass by some snipers.
   When she vented her air
   Through the holes that were there
She confounded the Cameron Pipers.

42

A nostalgic storm-trooper named Schmidt
Used a Nazi sex practices kit
   Which had boots and a whip
   With a nice metal tip
And his bride didn't like it a bit!

43

A pubescent girl scout of Dewar
Was raped by two cops and a brewer,
   A postman, three sailors,
   A shop-full of tailors,
And next week I will . . . *interview* her.

44

There was a young lady named Sentry
Who claimed to be raped by some gentry.
   But the judge said, 'Dismissed!!'
   When he looked where she pissed
There were no signs of forcible entry.

45

I came on a lady named Kitchener
As her lover was fucking the niche in her,
   So I pulled out my prick,
   And stuck it in quick
And buggered that son-of-a-bitch in her.

46

There was a young lady named Nance
Who had learned about sucking in France.
   And, when you'd insert it,
   She'd bite till she hurt it,
Then shove it right back in your pants.

47

To Sadie the touch of a male meant
An emotional cardiac ailment;
   And acuteness of breath
   Caused her untimely death
In the course of erotic impalement.

48

There was a young man of Balbriggan
Who was fearfully given to frigging,
   Till these noctural frolics
   Played hell with his bollox,
And killed the young man of Balbriggan.

49

An embalmer in ancient Karnak
Oozed it into a fresh corpse's crack.
  Rigor mortis set in
  And clamped off what had been
His pride, nor did he get it back.

50

When she wanted a new way to futter
He greased her behind with some butter;
  Then, with a sock,
  In went his jock,
And they carried her home on a shutter.

51

There was a young lady named White
Found herself in a terrible plight:
  A mucker named Tucker
  Had struck her, the fucker –
The bugger, the bastard, the shite!

52

There was a young lady of Rhyl
In an omnibus was taken ill.
  So she called the conductor,
  Who got in and fucked her,
Which did her more good than a pill.

53

There was a young girl of Penzance
Who boarded a bus in a trance.
  The passengers fucked her,
  Likewise the conductor.
The driver shot off in his pants.

54

There was a young lady named Gloria
Who was had by Sir Gerald du Maurier,
   And then by six men,
   Sir Gerald again,
And the band at the Waldorf-Astoria.

55

Quoth the coroner's jury in Preston,
'The verdict is rectal congestion.'
   They found an eight-ball
   On a shoemaker's awl
Halfway up the major's intestine.

56

Since the boys found no joys in her lap,
She chopped off her big brother's tap.
   At his death she did not repent,
   But fixed it with cement
And wore it in place with a strap.

57

A neurotic young man of Kildare
Drilled a hole in the seat of a chair.
   He fucked it all night,
   Then died of the fright
That maybe he wasn't 'all there'.

58

There was a young man of Savannah
Met his end in a curious manner.
   He diddled a hole
   In a telegraph pole
And electrified his banana.

59

When she danced at the Easter Parade,
Such a sexy impression she made
   That some lads from St Paul's,
   In tight jeans, hurt their balls
And had to be given first-aid.

60

There was a young singer named Springer,
Got his testicles caught in the wringer.
   He hollered with pain
   As they rolled down the drain
(*falsetto*): 'There goes my career as a singer!'

61

There was an old rake from Stamboul
Felt his ardour grow suddenly cool.
   No lack of affection
   Reduced his erection –
But his zipper got caught in his tool.

62

A horny young fellow named Redge
Was jerking off under a hedge.
   The gardener drew near
   With a huge pruning shear,
And trimmed off the edge of his wedge.

63

There was an old man from New York
Whose tool was as dry as a cork.
   While attempting to screw
   He split it in two,
And now his tool is a fork.

64

There was a young man of Malacca
Who always slept on his left knacker.
　　One Saturday night
　　He slept on his right,
And his knacker went off like a cracker.

65

There was a young man of Madras
Who was fucking a girl in the grass,
　　But the tropical sun
　　Spoiled half of his fun
By singeing the hair off his ass.

66

An accident really uncanny
Occurred to my elderly Granny:
　　She sat down in a chair
　　While her false teeth lay there
And bit herself right in the fanny.

67

There was a young fellow named Puttenham
Whose tool caught in doors upon shuttin' 'em.
　　He said, 'Well, perchance,
　　It would help to wear pants,
If I just could remember to button 'em.'

68

Did you hear about young Henry Lockett?
He was blown down the street by a rocket.
　　The force of the blast
　　Blew his balls up his ass,
And his pecker was found in his pocket.

69

A crooner who lived in Lahore
Got his balls caught in a door.
   Now his mezzo soprano
   Is rather piano
Though he was a loud basso before.

70

A virgin felt urged in Toulouse
Till she thought she would try self-abuse.
   In search of a hard on
   She ran out in the garden,
And was had by a statue of Zeus.

71

There was a young Scotchman named Jock
Who had the most horrible shock:
   He once took a shit
   In a leaf-covered pit,
And the crap sprung a trap on his cock.

72

There was a young student from Yale
Who was getting his first piece of tail.
   He shoved in his pole,
   But in the wrong hole,
And a voice from beneath yelled: 'No sale!'

73

There was a young lady named Nance
Who had ants in the seat of her pants.
   When they bit on her bottom
   She yelled, 'Jesus, God rot 'em!
I can't do the St Vitus dance.'

74

There was a young lady named Lea
Whose favours were frequent and free,
    And pants-pigeons flew
    Where her gooseberries grew,
And some of them flew on to me.

Smells and Horrors

❦

1

There once was a fellow named Howells
Had a terrible time with his bowels.
   His wife, so they say,
   Cleaned them out every day
With special elongated trowels.

2

A pathetic old maid of Bordeaux
Fell in love with a dashing young beau.
   To arrest his regard
   She would squat in his yard
And appealingly pee in the snow.

3

A person of most any nation
If afflicted with bad constipation,
   Can shove a cuirass
   Up the crack of his ass,
But it isn't a pleasing sensation.

4

The Rajah of Afghanistan
Imported a Birmingham can
   Which he set as a throne
   On a great Buddha stone –
But he crapped out of doors like a man

5

There was a young girl of Connecticut
Who didn't care much about etiquette.
  Whenever she was able
  She'd piss on the table
And mop off her cunt with her petticoat.

6

There was a young man from Australia
Who painted his arse like a dahlia.
  The colour was fine;
  Likewise the design.
But the perfume: ah, that was a failure!

7

In the garden remarked Lord Larkeeding:
'A fig for your digging and weeding.
  I like watching birds,
  While they're dropping their turds,
And spying on guinea pigs breeding.'

8

A flatulent nun of Hawaii
One Easter eve supped on papaya,
  Then honoured the Passover
  By turning her ass over
And obliging with Handel's *Messiah*.

9

There once was a vicar of Ryhill
Who went for a shit on a high hill;
  When his curate asked: 'Was it
  A goodly deposit?'
He said, '*Vox et praeterea nihil.*'

10

There was a young man of Loch Leven
Who went for a walk about seven.
   He fell into a pit
   That was brimful of shit,
And now the poor bugger's in heaven.

11

And then there's a story that's fraught
With disaster – of balls that got caught
   When a chap took a crap
   In the woods, and a trap
Underneath . . . Oh, I can't bear the thought!

12

There was a fat lady of Bryde
Whose shoelaces once came untied.
   She didn't dare stoop
   For fear she would poop,
And she cried and she cried and she cried.

13

There was a young lady called Alice
Who peed in a Catholic chalice.
   The padre agreed
   It was done out of need,
And not out of Protestant malice.

14

There was a young lady of Ealing
Who had a peculiar feeling.
   She lay on her back,
   And opened her crack,
And pissed from the floor to the ceiling.

15

I dined with the Duchess of Lee,
Who asked 'Do you fart when you pee?'
  I said with some wit:
  'Do you belch when you shit?'
And felt it was one up to me.

16

There was a young lady named Skinner,
Who dreamt that her lover was in her.
  She woke with a start,
  And let out a fart
Which was followed by luncheon and dinner.

17

Dr Johnson, when sober or pissed,
Could be frequently heard to insist,
  Letting out a great fart,
  'Yes, I follow Descartes –
I stink, and I therefore exist.'

18

An unfortunate fellow named Chase
Thought his arse was in quite the wrong place;
  And he showed indignation
  When investigation
Showed some people do fart through their face.

Spurred on by a very high wager
With an envious major named Bagier
  He proceeded to fart
  The complete oboe part
Of a Haydn octet in A major.

19

There was a young lady of Purdbright
Who never could quite get her turd right.
  She'd go to the closet
  And leave a deposit
Like a mouse or a bat or a bird might.

20

There was a young fellow called Cager,
Who, as the result of a wager,
  Offered to fart
  The whole oboe part
Of Mozart's *Quartet in F Major*.

21

A prisoner in Château d'If
Ran around on all fours for a sniff
  Of his comrade's posterior,
  And said, 'It's inferior,
But somehow reminds me of qif.'

22

A genteel young lady named Dexter
Found her husband exceedingly vexed her,
  For whenever they'd start
  He'd unfailingly fart
With a blast that damn nearly unsexed her.

23

There was a young girl of La Plata
Who was widely renowned as a farter.
  Her deafening reports
  At the Argentine Sports
Made her much in demand as a starter.

24

There was a young fellow from Sparta
A really magnificent farter,
   On the strength of one bean
   He'd fart *God Save the Queen*
And Beethoven's *Moonlight Sonata*.

25

There was a young Royal Marine
Who tried to fart *God Save the Queen*.
   When he reached the soprano
   Out came the guano
And his breeches weren't fit to be seen.

26

There was an old man who could piss
Through a ring – and, what's more, never miss.
   People came by the score
   And bellowed: '*Encore!*
Won't you do it again, sir? *Bis! Bis!*'

27

There was a young fellow named Fritz
Who planted an acre of tits.
   They came up in the fall,
   Pink nipples and all,
And he chewed them all up into bits.

28

There was a young man of Rangoon
Who farted and filled a balloon.
   The balloon went so high
   That it stuck in the sky,
And stank out the Man in the Moon.

29

There was a young lass of Blackheath
Who frigged an old man with her teeth.
   She complained that he stunk
   Not so much from the spunk,
But his arsehole was just underneath.

30

There was an old fellow of Brest
Who sucked off his wife with a zest.
   Despite her great howls
   He sucked out her bowels,
And spat them all over her chest.

31

There was an old woman of Ghent
Who swore that her cunt had no scent.
   She got fucked so often
   At last she got rotten,
And didn't she stink when she spent?

32

There was an old harlot of Wick
Who was sucking a coal-heaver's prick.
   She said, 'I don't mind
   The coal-dust and grime,
But the smell of your balls makes me sick.'

33

There was an old man of Tantivy
Who followed his son to the privy.
   He lifted the lid
   To see what he did,
And found that it smelt of Capivi.

34

There was a young man of the Tweed
Who sucked his wife's arse thro' a reed.
   When she had diarrhoea,
   He'd let none come near,
For fear they should poach on his feed.

35

There was a young lady of Newcastle
Who wrapped up a turd in a parcel,
   And sent it to a relation
   With this invitation –
'It has just come out hot from my arsehole.'

36

There was a young man of Newcastle,
Who tied up a shit in a parcel,
   And sent it to Spain
   With a note to explain
That it came from his grandmother's arsell.

37

There was an old person of Delhi
Awoke with a pain in his belly,
   And to cure it, 'tis said,
   He shit in his bed,
And the sheets were uncommonly smelly.

38

A nasty old bugger of Cheltenham
Once shit in his bags as he knelt in 'em.
   So he sold 'em at Ware
   To a gentleman there
Who didn't much like what he smelt in 'em.

39

A cabman who drove in Biarritz
Once frightened a fare into fits.
   When reprov'd for a fart,
   He said, 'God bless my heart,
When I break wind I usually shits.'

40

There was a young man of Bhogat,
The cheeks of whose ass were so fat
   That they had to be parted
   Whenever he farted,
And propped wide apart when he shat.

41

There was a young girl in Ohio
Whose baptismal name was Maria.
   She would put on airs
   And pee on the stairs,
If she thought that no one was nigh 'er.

42

There was a young lady of Pinner,
Who dreamt that her lover was in her.
   This excited her heart,
   So she let a great fart,
And shit out her yesterday's dinner.

43

There was an old fellow from Roop
Who'd lost all control of his poop.
   One evening at supper
   His wife said, 'Now, Tupper,
Stop making that noise with your soup!'

44

There was a young man from Kilbride
Who fell into a shit house and died.
  His heartbroken brother
  Fell into another,
And now they're interred side by side.

45

A mannerly fellow named Phyfe
Was greatly distressed by his wife,
  For whene'er she was able
  She'd shit on the table,
And gobble the shit – with her knife!

46

There was a young lady of Totten
Whose tastes grew perverted and rotten.
  She cared not for steaks,
  Or for pastry and cakes,
But lived upon penis *au gratin*.

47

A horrid old lady of Summit,
Every time she got laid had to vomit,
  And although she would groan
  When her man got a bone,
'Give it here,' she would say, 'and I'll gum it.'

48

A fellatrix's healthful condition
Proved the value of spunk as nutrition.
  Her remarkable diet
  (I suggest that you try it)
Was only her clients' emission.

49

There once was a baker of Nottingham
Who in making eclairs would put snot in 'em.
   When he ran out of snot,
   He would, like as not,
Take his pecker and jack off a shot in 'em.

50

There were two little mice in Rangoon
Who sought lunch in an old lady's womb.
   Cried one mouse, 'By Jesus,
   I'll wager this cheese is
As old as the cheese in the moon!'

51

There was a young fellow of Perth,
The nastiest bastard on earth,
   When his wife was confined
   He pulled down the blind
And ate up the whole afterbirth.

52

An elderly rabbi named Riskin
Dines daily on cunt-juice and foreskin,
   And to further his bliss,
   At dessert he'll drink piss,
For which he is always a'thirstin'.

53

There was an old man of Corfu
Who fed upon cunt-juice and spew.
   When he couldn't get that,
   He ate what he shat –
And bloody good shit he shat, too.

On clinkers his choice often fell,
Or clabbered piss brought to a jell.
　　When these palled to his taste
　　He tried snot and turd-paste,
And found them delicious as well.

He ate them, and sighed, and said, 'What
Uncommonly fine shit and snot!
　　Now really, the two
　　Are too good to be true –
I would rather have ate them than not.'

54

There once was a midget named Carr
Who couldn't reach up to the bar,
　　So in every saloon
　　He climbed a spittoon
And guzzled his liquor from thar.

55

There was a young man named Morel
Who played with his prick till he fell.
　　When to get up he started
　　He suddenly farted,
And fell down again from the smell.

56

There was a young man had the art
Of making a capital tart
　　With a handful of shit,
　　Some snot and a spit,
And he'd flavour the whole with a fart.

57

There was an old maid from Shalott
Who lived upon frog shit and snot.
   When she tired of these
   She would eat the green cheese
That she scraped from the sides of her twat.

58

There was a young man of King's Cross
Who amused himself frigging a horse,
   Then licking the spend
   Which still dripped from the end,
Said, 'It tastes just like anchovy sauce.'

59

There was a young man from Marseilles
Who lived on clap juice and snails.
   When tired of these
   He lived upon cheese
From his prick, which he picked with his nails.

60

A young lady who once had a Jew beau
Found out soon that he'd got a bubo,
   So when it was ripe
   She put in a pipe
And sucked up the juice through a tube oh!

61

There was a young lady, and what do you think?
She said, 'I care nought for a prick that don't stink,
   And I think that a fuck
   Ain't so good as a suck
When you've pulled back the foreskin and uncovered
   the pink.'

62

There was an old man of Kentucky,
Said to his old woman, 'Oi'll fuck ye.'
    She replied, 'Now you wunt
    Come anigh my old cunt,
For your prick is all stinking and mucky.'

63

A young man from famed Chittagong
Worked hard at a stool and worked long.
    He felt a hard mass
    Obstructing his ass,
Then shit and cried, 'I shit a gong!'

64

There was an old man of Seringapatam
Besmeared his wife's anus with raspberry jam,
    Then licked off the sweet,
    And pronounced it a treat,
And for public opinion he cared not a damn.

65

A plump English prof from Atlanta
Was bloated with bawdy, bold banter.
    He'd sit on his ass
    And let fly his gas
Whenever he sniffed a decanter.

66

There was an aesthetic young miss
Who thought it the apex of bliss
    To jazz herself silly
    With the bud of a lily,
Then go to the garden and piss.

67

An unfortunate bugger named Cowl
Took a shit while as drunk as an owl.
   He stumbled, alack!
   And fell flat on his back,
And his bollocks slipped into his bowel.

68

The intestines of Dante Rossetti
Were exceedingly fragile and petty.
   All he could eat
   Was finely chopped meat,
And all he could shit was spaghetti.

69

There was a young mate of a lugger,
Who took out a girl just to hug her.
   'I've my monthlies,' she said,
   'And a cold in the head,
But my bowels work well . . . do you bugger?'

70

An alluring young shoat of Paree
Fills all of her suitors with glee,
   For when they implore
   Her to give a bit more,
She invariably answers, 'Wee, wee.'

71

There was a young man from the Coast
Who received a parcel by post.
   It contained, so I heard,
   A triangular turd
And the balls of his grandfather's ghost.

72

A daughter of fair Ioway,
While at sport in the toilet one day,
   Swallowed some of her pee,
   'And hereafter,' said she,
'I'll do it at lunch every day.'

Death

❦

1

A maiden at college named Breeze,
Weighed down by BA's and Litt D's,
   Collapsed from the strain.
   Alas, it was plain,
She was killing herself by degrees.

2

Said a butcher's apprentice from Frome
Who aspired to be bride (and not groom),
   'With some knives from the shop,
   I shall do my own op.'
And these words are inscribed on his tomb.

3

There was a young man who said, 'Ayer
Has answered the atheist's prayer.
   For a hell one can't verify
   Surely can't terrify –
At least, till you know you are there.'

4

There was a young driver named Jake
Who made the most stupid mistake:
   He drove through the wall
   And into the hall,
When he mixed up the gas and the brake.

5

There was a young man of South Bray
Making fireworks one summer day.
   He dropped his cigar
   In the gunpowder jar . . .
There WAS a young man of South Bay

6

A new servant-maid named Maria
Had trouble lighting the fire.
   The wood being green,
   She used gasoline . : .
Her position by now is much higher.

7

A skeleton once in Khartoum
Invited a ghost to his room.
   They spent the whole night
   In the eeriest fight
As to who should be frightened of whom.

8

Astute Melanesians on Munda
Heard a parson discussing the wunda
   Of Virginal Birth –
   They debated its worth,
Then tore the poor padre asunda.

9

They've buried a salesman named Phipps.
He married, on one of his trips
   A widow named Block –
   Then died of the shock
When he found there were five little chips.

10

There once was a Countess of Ryde
Who swam too far out with the tide.
   Thought a man-eating shark:
   'How's this for a lark?
Have faith, and the Lord will provide.'

11

A fancy-meat packer named Young,
One day, when his nerves were unstrung,
   Pushed his wife's ma (unseen)
   In the chopping machine,
Then canned her and labelled her 'Tongue'.

12

Said a widow, whose singular vice
Was to keep her late husband on ice,
   'It's been hard since I lost him –
   I'll never defrost him!
Cold comfort, but cheap at the price.'

13

There was a young fellow called Hall
Who fell in the spring in the fall;
   'Twould have been a sad thing
   Had he died in the spring,
But he didn't, he died in the fall.

14

There was an old man in a hearse,
Who murmured, 'This might have been worse;
   Of course the expense
   Is simply immense,
But it doesn't come out of my purse.

15

There was a young man from Kilbride
Who fell down a sewer and died.
  Now he had a brother
  Who fell down another;
And now they're interred side by side.

16

There was a young man of Moose Jaw
Who wanted to meet Bernard Shaw.
  When they questioned him, 'Why?'
  He made no reply,
But sharpened an axe and a saw.

17

There was a young lady of Malta
Who strangled her aunt with a halter.
  She said, 'I won't bury her;
  She'll do for my terrier.
She'll keep for a month if I salt her.'

18

There was once an eccentric old boffin
Who remarked, in a fine fit of coughing,
  'It isn't the cough
  That carries you off,
But the coffin they carry you off in.'

19

There was a young man from the city
Who met what he thought was a kitty;
  He gave it a pat,
  And said! 'Nice little cat . . . '
They buried his clothes, out of pity.

20

A railway official at Crewe
Met an engine one day that he knew;
  Though he smiled and he bowed,
  That engine was proud:
It cut him – it cut him in two!

21

A daring young fellow in Bangor
Sneaked a super-swift jet from its hangar.
  When he crashed in the bay,
  Neighbours laid him away
In rather more sorrow than anger.

22

There was an old fellow named Hewing,
Whose heart stopped while he was a-screwing;
  He gasped: 'Really, miss,
  Don't feel bad about this –
There's nothing I'd rather die doing.'

23

If intercourse gives you thrombosis,
And continence causes neurosis,
  I'd rather expire
  Fulfilling desire
Than live in a state of psychosis.

24

There was a young fellow called Clyde
Who once at a funeral was spied.
  When asked who was dead,
  He smilingly said:
'I don't know – I just came for the ride.'

25

A young schizophrenic named Struther,
When told of the death of his brother,
  Said: 'Yes, it's too bad,
  But I can't feel too sad –
After all, I still have each other.'

26

Said a gleeful young man from Torbay:
'This is really a red-letter day;
  For I've poisoned with sherbert
  My rich Uncle Herbert
Because he had too much to say!'

27

There was a rash fellow called Weir,
Who hadn't an atom of fear;
  He indulged a desire
  To touch a live wire –
And any last line will do here.

28

There was a young fellow named Sistall,
Who shot three old maids with a pistol.
  When 'twas known what he'd done,
  He was given a gun
By the unmarried curates of Bristol.

29

There was a young fellow from Tyne
Put his head on the South-Eastern line;
  But he died of *ennui*,
  For the five fifty-three
Didn't come till a quarter past nine.

30

In the turbulent turgid St Lawrence
Fell a luscious young damsel named Florence,
   Where poor famished fish
   Made this beautiful dish
An object of utter abhorrence.

31

A daring young lady of Guam
Observed, 'The Pacific's so calm.
   I'll swim out for a lark.'
   She met a large shark,
'Let us now sing the Ninetieth Psalm.'

32

There was an old man who averred
He had learned how to fly like a bird;
   Cheered by thousands of people,
   He leapt from the steeple –
This tomb states the date it occurred.

33

A certain young gourmet of Crediton
Took some *pâté de foie gras* and spread it on
   A chocolate biscuit,
   Then murmured, 'I'll risk it.'
His tomb bears the date that he said it on.

34

There was once a schoolboy, named Hannibal,
Who won local fame as a cannibal
   By eating his mother,
   His father, his brother
And his two sisters, Gertrude and Annabelle.

35

There was a young man from Laconia,
Whose mother-in-law had pneumonia.
   He hoped for the worst
   And after March 1st
They buried her 'neath a begonia.

36

There was a young joker named Tarr,
Who playfully pickled his ma.
   When he finished his work,
   He remarked with a smirk,
'This will make quite a family jar.'

Index

The references in this index are to page numbers